OPEN
SHUTTERS

تمت الطباعة في بريطانيا العظمى في 2010
من قبل شركة ترولي المحدودة
www.trolleybooks.com

حقوق الطبع للصور والنصوص المرافقة محفوظة للمصورات ومشروع العدسات المفتوحة ولـ
Index on Censorship
لعام 2009

حقوق الطبع للمقدمات محفوظة لأرادة الجبوري ويوجيني دولبرغ وميسون الباجةجي
اخراج الكتاب: يوجيني دولبرغ وجيجي جانوتزي

الاخراج الفني: مارتن و واي
www.fruitmachinedesign.com

اخراج النص: يوجيني دولبرغ، ميسون الباجةجي، هانا واطسون
الترجمة: نوارة محفوظ، ميسون الباجةجي، نادبا حمدان قطان

ليوجيني دولبرغ حق التعريف ككاتبة لهذا الكتاب وفقاً لقانون حقوق الطبع والتصميم وبراءة
الاختراع لعام 1998

سجل دليل هذا الكتاب في المكتبة البريطانية

ISBN 978-1-904563-99-0

طبع في ايطاليا 2010 في مطابع
Grafiche Antiga

رأى هذا المشروع النور بفضل مساندة
Index on Censorship
وتمويل
UNDP, Ministerio de Asuntos Exteriores y de Cooperacion and
Agencia Española de Cooperacion Internacional

نال الكتاب دعماً سخياً من
Prince Claus Fund

**Prince Claus
Fund Library**

للمزيد من المعلومات حول معرض العدسات المفتوحة في العراق برجى الاتصال بـ
eugeniedolberg@gmail.com

للمزيد من المعلومات حول الفيلم الوثائقي
(مشاعرنا التقطت الصور: عدسات مفتوحة في العراق)
ميسون الباجةجي
برجى التفضل بزيارة
www.oxymoronfilms.com

This book is a collection of individual photographs and photographic essays made by women from Baghdad, Basra, Falluja, Kirkuk and Mosul in 2006/7. These women were not photographers or writers, but were brought together by their need to tell their stories.

INTRODUCTION

In the aftermath of 2003, Iraq was left without an effective government or civilian infrastructure and its people became increasingly vulnerable to the arbitrary violence of those exploiting the chaos. By 2006 so many journalists had been targeted and killed or kidnapped that it had become almost impossible to work and the sources of news from Iraq were largely military and governmental. The story of what was happening to ordinary people in Iraq was not being heard.

At that time I was living in bordering Syria. I had been working for many years internationally as a photographer and had become frustrated with the increasingly corporate nature of the media. It demanded stories, which had little to do with the concerns that motivated me, or even the type of photography that moved me. On the other hand, I felt deeply privileged to be in contact with so many inspirational people on a daily basis. The more time I spent away from Europe and USA, the more I realised how much interference, often in the guise of aid, there was in the affairs of other countries, leaving people with neither a sense of ownership of their own history or a role to play in determining the direction of their country's future. I became aware of how flawed and narrow the dominating ideas shaping foreign policy and development were. The system by which information was gathered and interpreted made no sense to me. Why should the interpretation of a foreigner flying into a region for a few weeks, be privileged over the understanding which people have about their own society?

In Damascus, I met many Iraqis who'd fled. I was repeatedly stunned by the magnitude and often surreal nature of the violence they described, and the extreme lengths to which people had been forced to go in order to survive. One man rolled up his sleeve and showed me his name, address and phone number tattooed on his arm; if he was killed and his body thrown on the street or he was blown up in an explosion, or beheaded, he could be identified and his body returned to his family. It had become common practice, he told me.

I also heard, again and again, of the enduring courage, determination and activism of women in Iraq. In 26 years of almost continuous war and 13 years of the most savage sanctions in history, Iraqi women had been sustaining the society while their men were fighting. They were the breadwinners; they kept their families together – and all this while dealing with the psychological fallout from a generation of Iraqi men whose whole youth was spent at war. Since 2003, they had been battling to hang on to hard won constitutional rights, which conservative religious parties were trying to reverse - basic rights relating to inheritance, marriage, divorce and child custody.

In London, along with millions of others, I had demonstrated against the war. As a British citizen I felt the enormous weight of what my government was doing in Iraq and a responsibility to help make a record of what was happening. I decided to do a participatory photography project, Open Shutters Iraq, with a group of Iraqi women. It was not going to be about making beautiful pictures, but about taking photographs that expressed what they wanted to say and how they felt; about communicating experience, not only events.

I remember my first phone conversation with Irada al Jabbouri, the Iraqi project manager in Baghdad. She took leave from her job to work on Open Shutters Iraq and at great personal risk travelled around the country, using a range of IDs and disguises, to find the women who would participate in the project. "This is not a project" she told me, "This is a dream, a dream I want to live for my daughter, so she can grow up and understand what is truly happening now".

It was impossibly dangerous to do the work in Iraq itself, but Syria was a feasible alternative. There the women could come from Iraq to learn photography and share their experiences before returning home to shoot their photo-stories.

We lived and worked together in a traditional house in the Old City in Damascus. The women came from all over Iraq and had no previous photographic experience. I realised that before starting to make photo-stories, the women needed to have the space, trust and creative tools to reflect on their lives. This process began by telling them about my life, the personal experiences which had made me who I was today. I wanted to establish a sense of equality, trust and openness.

I will never forget the morning I asked them to make blind lifelines. We put on some gentle *oud* music and, pens in hand, they closed their eyes. The room was charged with emotion as they tried to recall every moment of their lives and consider how they had been affected. I walked around the tables watching their faces and bodies change with the line they were drawing, their hands stiffen and tense as the line went down – a particularly traumatic memory – and their shoulders and forehead relax with recollections of happier times. Each of them was somehow isolated in her darkness with only the sound of marker pens scratching across paper to remind her of the presence of others. Without words I saw them travel through wars, sanctions, broken marriages, grief, love, happiness, times of resistance, achievements and small triumphs. Eventually the lifelines evolved into full 'life maps' with scrawled poems, observations, quotes and personal snapshots. I asked each woman to present her 'life map' to the other participants. Although most of the women had always lived in Iraq, this was the first time they could listen to others from such a diversity of social, religious and political backgrounds. I was nervous and wondered if dialogues might instead become raging arguments. Although there were moments of tension, everyone tried to respect each other and I watched the women's faces as they listened to each other full of patience and compassion.

I had lived in the Middle East for some time, but nothing had prepared me for the stories I heard. Everything I thought about Iraq was shattered. I had no idea of the severity of the Iraqi experience in the last few decades; no one had escaped unspeakable loss and trauma and no one had had a moment to recover.

Everyday, they would also study different elements of photography, go out into the alleyways of the Old City to shoot and review their photos later in a slide show. There was an urgency to master all the techniques of photography and to use to say what they wanted.

When the time came to return to Iraq, they had decided on a subject to shoot. Their choice of stories was bold, intimate.

On the logistics form, the women were asked how they would protect themselves and minimise risk; several of them wrote the same answer: "I will leave it to the will of God". This caused a lot of laughter at the time. It wasn't quite what I'd expected, but finally their point was crystal clear. When the world around you is falling apart, whatever precautions you take or preparations you make, in the end it's completely out of your hands.

Death threats (unrelated to the project), militia kidnappings, bombings, curfews and border closures were among the obstacles bravely overcome during the six weeks of shooting in Iraq – not to speak of the power cuts, road closures, petrol queues, lack of water and blocked telephone networks that were part of daily life. Despite all of this, when the time came for editing, small groups of the women arrived back in Damascus with huge amounts of shot material, which they edited and wrote about in five-day workshops.

Their stories are a unique witness to the human crisis that is hidden behind the news reports where people just become numbers. They are a testimony to the bravery of a group of women living through the unthinkable horror that the invasion of Iraq had become.

I would like to thank Index on Censorship for their dedicated support, United Nations Development Programme for funding the project and the Prince Claus Fund and kind donor who prefers to remain anonymous for financing the publication of this book.

I would like to thank the project manager in Syria, my translator and dear friend, Nawara Mahfoud, Maysoon Pachachi, who made a film about the project and whose support and friendship was invaluable and changed the very nature of the project, and Irada Al Jabbouri whose courage and strength inspired us all.

I would also like to thank all the other people who helped to make this project possible, who are too numerous to name. And, finally, my heartfelt gratitude and love to the women who came from Iraq to tell their stories.

I write this in memory of two of them, Sajida, Um Mohammed, who we have lost to the effects of depleted uranium and a shattered Iraqi health service and Sarwa, who was killed in Mosul by an armed group targeting vocal women.

Eugenie Dolberg
Tehran, 2010

ETCHED IN WORDS AND IMAGES

My daughter sleeps in her bed, while I sit at the table writing, in the heart of an enchanted city of beauty and calm. I question a woman called Irada, who lives in a country called Iraq in 2006/7. She says 'I don't want to place life in the coffin of language', even though I did try to say what was happening at that time and place. We had to speak, then, in a context where you only heard gunshots, the blast of car bombs, roar of fighter planes and the shouting of politicians with their militias, and the media for whom we were numbers, erased in every new broadcast, only to be replaced by new ones. Was it bravery that made us try to speak? No, definitely not... it was fear that brought us together...a fear that this moment would pass as so many others have passed over the decades, without our having said what happened. We were afraid that we would end up as individuals, just talking about ourselves to the Other, and not about our collective experience; the Other who, at a certain point in time, had control over what was being said.

I spent months trying to find the women. Once my friend, Yahya Al Kubaisi convinced the families of two of the participants from Falluja that I was of good character, I was able to talk to them about the project. I assured them it was not linked to any political organisation and had no suspect funding. This all had to take place over a period of days via constantly and suddenly disconnected telephone conversations. At the time, access to Falluja was denied to anyone who was not from there. I almost lost my mind when I suddenly realised that Mariam's passport would expire two weeks before the project was due to begin. Renewing the passport required her to get new identity documents - the old ones had been burned in the first attack on Falluja in April 2004 - and then we had to find a way to get those documents to Baghdad.

My neighbour Luma's friend, who lived in Kirkuk, suggested Niran. I went to meet her and her family, and she was ready to travel with us to Syria and her family accepted. A while later, though, her 20 year-old sister and 5 year-old nephew, Sinan, were killed in an explosion in a street market and that destroyed Niran's desire for life. My friend, Narmin Al Mufti, in Kirkuk, suggested Lu'lu'a as a replacement.

I travelled to Mosul with forged ID papers and prayed I would not need to use them. My heart sank when I saw my friend, Bushra Bustani's house, its windows blown out and its doors hanging on their hinges; a car bomb had gone off two streets away only the day before. She was to take me to meet a potential participant and her family, but I was too embarrassed to ask that of her in the present circumstances. We cleared up the shattered glass in a corner of the kitchen and spent the night drinking tea, wrapped in blankets and huddling around the kerosene stove. We reminisced about our trip to Beirut in 1992, full of mishap and comic misadventure – trying to avoid talking about the violence, which was overwhelming Iraq like a bulldozer without brakes. At dawn I returned to Baghdad without having met Betool's family. It was pointless to go see them without having someone to introduce and vouch for me – especially since the stories of Iraqi women being trafficked were all over the media.

It was the women who found me and not the other way around. I hesitated to choose Sarwa; I tried to discover shared expectations of the project. During our third phone conversation, she said she couldn't stop dreaming about the project and she wasn't just dreaming for herself, but also for her mother. Her words convinced me that I wanted her on the project. I asked her to find a partner from Mosul, where she lived, and she chose Antoinette, who I accepted immediately.

I first saw Lujane at Baghdad University, in the middle of a vehement verbal attack on a man, whose only response was silence. A few days later, I saw her again and invited her into my office. I told her about the project; she was interested and suggested Sarab, who she contacted right there and then; she was painting the walls of her brother's house where she lives.

There were 3 women in Basra who were keen to participate in the project, but one by one they all had to drop out for different reasons. Finally I found Noor through the father of one of the women I had approached. She introduced me to Hana', a hairdresser who still managed to keep her salon open even though intense militia violence had enveloped the city in depression. From the salon we went to meet Hana's widowed mother, but she doubted that Hana's uncles would ever allow her to travel without being accompanied by someone else from the family. The mother and daughter hatched a plan. They would say that Hana' was going on a pilgrimage to the Sayida Zeinab shrine in Damascus and while there, she would buy a tattoo machine to use in her salon. I promised to help and asked Raya, a participant from Baghdad, to arrange for Hana' to learn tattooing in Damascus in her free time.

Winter 2006. People were leaving Baghdad in unprecedented numbers; you had to book your flight at least a month in advance. The women from Kirkuk and Mosul flew from the airport in Erbil. The two from Falluja preferred to go by road to Damascus, rather than risking the trip to Baghdad in order to fly from there. And as for those of us coming from Baghdad, we had to travel south to Basra by road in order to fly back north to Damascus. 18 hours before our flight, Hana' phoned saying that she couldn't join us because her brother in Baghdad had been forced out of his house and had returned to the family home in Basra, and now it was impossible for her to come with us. Just as I was about to give up on finding another particpant from Basra, my friend Muwaffaq Al Rifa'i suggested Sajida, Um Mohammed. As soon as I met her, I knew this is who I'd been searching for.

Yes, indeed, it was not me who found them, but they who found me; so that they could finally tell their stories and move on. They etched them in words and images during the days we spent together. Sarwa and Um Mohammed have passed on and their stories have ended, while the others are still writing theirs, in a country rushing headlong towards obliteration.

Irada Al Jabbouri
Iraqi Project Manager
Istanbul, 2009

A FORM OF RESISTANCE

I am a London-based filmmaker, Iraqi by origin, and by the time Eugenie first talked to me in the summer of 2006 about filming the Open Shutters Iraq project, I had made two other documentaries about the country.

I arrived in Damascus in December, with my camera and no crew and began filming. I soon saw what was different about Eugenie's approach. From the beginning, she emphasised the importance of the emotional content of the image – yes, you had to learn about light and composition, but without emotion, a photograph was just a picture. She tried to get the women to 'think emotionally'; to identify what a photo expressed or made them feel, to discover what they wanted to express in their own photographs.

The 'life maps' were the turning point. As the women listened to each other – spellbound – their own stories and experiences began surfacing, were recognised and 'remembered'. In the end, the women, each with the thread of her life in her hand, had woven together a fabric of the collective experience of Iraqi women over the past few decades. The process was dynamic and transformative, occurring within the context of a creative project where something, which would communicate to others, could be made. The work the Open Shutters participants produced was remarkable for its emotional force and clarity.

During the 1991 Gulf War, like so many other Iraqis outside the country, I sat night after night watching TV; the 'fireworks' exploding in Baghdad's night sky and the 'smart' bombs taking out their targets as if in some video game. I was traumatised to the point of losing my grip on the English language, which I had spoken all my life. Words became separated from their meanings and I struggled to remember names of the most ordinary objects – 'table', 'salt', 'window'... but maybe what was really being lost was the ability to speak about the loss – to mourn, in fact. I finally, however, found my voice by making a film about Iraq and, at that point, I began to understand that you sometimes try to repair, in creative work, what has been shattered in the 'real world'.

I think for all of us, the women taking their photographs and writing their texts, and for me making my film, this was a form of resistance, an assertion of existence in the face of all that was being un-made – both inside and outside us.

Maysoon Pachachi
Filmmaker
London, 2010

CHRONOLOGY

Year	
3500 BC	BCE Sumerian civilisation in what is now south-eastern Iraq
633 AD	Muslim conquest of Iraq
680	Imam Hussein, who became the most important figure in Shia Islam murdered in Kerbala in central Iraq
762	Foundation of Baghdad, the new capital of the Abbasid Caliphate rulers of the Muslim world
945 – 1225	Persian and Turkish invasions and conquests of Iraq
1258	Mongol armies under Hulago invade Baghdad
	The Tigris runs black with the ink of the looted libraries
1347	Bubonic plague decimates the population
1401	Tamerlaine, the Mongol conqueror, sacks Baghdad
1508	Baghdad conquered by the Safavids of Persia
1534	Iraq conquered by the Ottoman Turks
1914 - 1918	First World War and the Arab revolt against the Ottoman Empire
1916	Secret Sykes-Picot Agreement between Britain and France dividing up the Middle East into spheres of influence
1920	British mandate over Iraq established popular rebellion in the south of the country against British rule
1921	Feisal I crowned first King of Iraq
1927	Discovery of oil in Kirkuk
1948	Uprising against British influence
1958	July 14th revolution establishing a republic
1963	First Ba'athist coup
1968	Second Ba'athist coup
1972	Nationalisation of the oil industry
1979	Saddam Hussein becomes president of Iraq
1980 - 1988	Iran-Iraq War
1990	Iraqi invasion of Kuwait
	The most comprehensive sanctions in history are imposed on Iraq
1991	US-led forces evict Iraqi army from Kuwait
	Uprisings against Saddam's rule are brutally put down
1997	Oil for Food Programme
1998	UN arms inspectors leave the country and a brief bomb attack by US forces
March 2003	US led forces invade Iraq
April 2003	US led forces enter Baghdad
	Iraq is placed under US and UK military occupation

On my way to college, I pass the time reading the black banners mourning those killed by all this madness and violence. They hang on the walls of houses and at the intersections of roads. I see this coffin on the taxi and I wonder how this person met their end. It rarely happens now that Iraqis die from old age or illness. I used to feel sad for families mourning their loved ones, but now if someone dies naturally, I think how lucky they are. Shamous, Baghdad

في طريقي إلى الجامعة أمضي الوقت في قراءة يافطات سود تنعى الذين سحقهم جنون العنف .. يافطات علقت على جدران البيوت وفي مفترقات الطرق.. ارى هذا التابوت واتسائل "ترى كيف مات هذا الشخص ؟ "صار من النادر أن يموت العراقي بمرض او لتقدمه في العمر . في السابق كنت اشعر بالحزن على العائلات التي تفقد احبتها اما الان فنقول ، ان سمعنا بموت احدهم بصورة طبيعية ، كم هم محظوظون أهله واحبته !! شموس - بغداد

Previous page
A while ago on the radio, they announced a campaign to beautify Baghdad. So, we expected the concrete barriers and barbed wire to be removed. We were surprised to see hundreds of Iraqi flags painted on the concrete walls instead. Lujane, Baghdad

الصفحة التالية
أعلن في الراديو منذ فترة عن حملة تجميل بغداد . توقعنا أن تزال الحواجز والأسلاك الشائكة، فوجئنا بالعلم العراقي مرسوما على كل الحواجز الكونكريتية. لجين - بغداد

I took this picture of my mum's and my shadows on the concrete barrier near my school. It's just next to the school guard's house that was blown up.
My mum goes everywhere with me.
Dima (age 6), Baghdad

أخذت صورة للخيال مالتي ومالت امي على حاجز يم
بيت حارس مدرستي اللي فجروا بيته.. أمي وياي بكل
مكان .. ديمة – بغداد

Our water was cut for six continuous days. I woke, stepped out of bed and found myself ankle-deep in water. One of my brothers, checking whether the water had been turned on, forgot to close a tap. Our carpets, mattresses, everything was utterly soaked. And several flats in our building were completely flooded. It seems we weren't the only ones who forgot to turn the taps off. Lujane, the building where I live, Baghdad

كانت المياه قد قطعت لستة أيام متواصلة .. استيقظت من النوم .. وضعت رجلي خارج السرير، كانت الأرضية مبتلة تماما.. كان احد أخوتي يتفقد عودة المياه المنقطعة ونسي الصنبور مفتوحا.. سجادنا وفرشنا وكل أشيائنا ابتلت ... بيدو اننا لسنا وحدنا من نسي الصنبور مفتوحا .. كان أكثر من بيت في العمارة غارقا !! لجين – البناية التي اسكن فيها – بغداد

Previous page
Electricity, oh electricity...Her Majesty has announced her arrival in our house – the bell we installed especially for that purpose just rang. My mother runs to turn on the washing machine and then the vacuum cleaner so she can hoover up our dreams scattered all over the house, with the ash of our cigarettes. My father switches on the iron hoping he can finish pressing his shirt, which hides in its fabric, the story of a life frayed by war, shock and the separation from loved ones. My sister, with her Sumerian eyes, turns on the radio – maybe she can hear Fairouz singing, "Beirut enjoys the glory of its ashes". Raya, Baghdad

الصفحة السابقة
الكهرباء ....الكهرباء ..أعلنت للبيت قدومها الجليل بجرس وضعناه خصيصا ليعلن الحدث السعيد.. وهاهي أمي تركض لتشغل غسالة الملابس وتسرع بعدها لتشغيل المكنسة الكهربائية لتلتقط أحلامنا التي تناثرت مع رماد سجائرنا . أبي يشغل المكواة أملا في أن يكمل كيَ قميصه الذي طوى مراراً بين أنسجته حكايات عمر تهرأ من كثرة الحروب والصدمات وفراق الأحبة ..أختي ذات العيون السومرية تشغل الراديو علها تسمع فيروز وهي تغني (لبيروت مجد من رماد)... ريا – بغداد

This pile of junk attracted my attention.
When I went to investigate, I found a
woman inside baking bread in a mud
oven. The Americans promised us
skyscrapers when they invaded, but
obviously, these have shrunk on the
way between New York and Falluja.
Tijan, in my city, Falluja

*March 13, 2007. Airplanes are hovering
in Falluja's sky; they're dropping bundles
of wooden logs by parachute. Thank
you America for state of the art heating
technology. Mariam*

لفتت انتباهي كومة الخردة هذه.. اقتربت، وجدت سيدة تخبز
على التنور.. وعدنا الأمريكان بناطحات سحاب عندما
دخلوا العراق.. يبدو أن ناطحات السحاب تتقزم في الطريق
بين نيويورك.. والفلوجة !! تيجان – الفلوجة

يوم 2007-3-31 حومت الطائرات في سماء الفلوجة
"وأهدتنا" حزما من الحطب.. شكرا "لأمريكا" لأنها
زودتنا بتقنيات حديثة للتدفئة !! مريم

My brother parked his car in front of our house...the Americans wanted to drive their Hummers down our street... the car was in their way...so they drove over it and crushed it...when we complained, they trotted out the same sentence they always do when they kill someone by mistake or damage a house..."we are so sorry, we are really very sorry"... Mariam, Falluja

When the Americans invaded Falluja, we didn't know whether we were crying for the dead or because we were afraid. Whenever I leave the house, I say farewell to my mother – it is as if we are all carrying our blood in a spoon – trying not to spill it. Mariam

أوقف أخي سيارته في باب دارنا، أراد الأمريكان بهمراتهم
المرور في شارعنا، أزعجهم وجود السيارة.. ساروا عليها..
هشموها.. لكنهم وللحقيقة لم ينسوا، عندما احتججنا على
سلوكهم، أن يقولوا جملتهم المعتادة . كلما قتلوا شخصا
بالخطأ او دمروا بيتا او أي ممتلكات
"we are so sorry, we are really very sorry"
مريم – الفلوجة

عندما اجتاح الأمريكان الفلوجة، لم نكن ندري ان كنا
نبكي الموتى أم نبكي خوفا .كنت كلما غادرت البيت اسلم
على أمي سلام الوداع ..كنا كمن يحمل دمه بملعقة .مريم

Since the beginning of the occupation, the life of minorities has been fraught with danger. I am Mandaean and there are now only a few thousand of us left in the country...like many other Iraqis we've been displaced, kidnapped and forced to leave...in some places our graves have been violated, women have been forced to cover their heads...On her wedding day, my friend Areej insisted on all the proper rituals, determined to feel a bit of happiness.
Shamous, Baghdad

"$100,000 to get your son back...otherwise, you'll find him on your doorstep – hacked to pieces in a garbage bag". My father went to deliver the ransom money in the Thawra area - there was intense fighting that night between the militias and the Americans. He came back without my brother. There was a curfew. We spent the night walking the streets with our neighbours calling his name...he was 12 years old...we were afraid they would throw him on the street and the dogs would attack him. Shamous

منذ الاحتلال صارت حياة الأقليات في العراق محفوفة بالمخاطر.. انا صابئية ولم يتبق منا سوى بضعة الاف ... ومثل الكثير من العراقين تعرضنا للتهجير والاختطافات .. درست قبورنا في مناطق وفرض على النساء ارتداء الحجاب.. أصرت صديقتي اريج على الفرح فقامت بكل طقوس العرس ومراسيمه.
شموس – بغداد

"نريد ميت ألف دولار.. نعطيك ابنك وإذا ما تدفع باجر تلقاه مكطع بجيس زبالة على بابك". طلبوا من والدي تسليم المبلغ في حي الثورة.. وكانت المعارك مشتعلة بين جيش المهدي والأمريكان.. عاد ولم يكن اخي معه.. كان منع التجول معلنا.. قضينا الليل نمشي مع الجيران في الشوارع ونصرخ باسمه.. كان في الثانية عشر من عمره .. خفنا ان يرموه في الشارع وتهاجمه الكلاب شموس

If someone is not home by 5pm and you cannot reach them by phone, everybody in the family is paralyzed with fear and the image of their body riddled with bullets and thrown on a rubbish heap. The only time we can breathe again and relax is when we are back together under one roof. And if we are lucky enough to get one hour of electricity, we all gather together in front of the TV. Sarab, Baghdad

يتملكنا الرعب اذا ما تأخر احد افراد الأسرة في العودة الى البيت قبل الخامسة مساء واخفقنا في التواصل معه هاتفيا . تطبق علينا صورة العثور عليه مقتولا ومرميا على مكب للنفايات في اليوم التالي ولا نلتقط انفاسنا حتى يعود الجميع ونجلس تحت سقف واحد واذا ما حالفنا الحظ ومنوا علينا بساعة كهرباء نتجمع امام التلفاز

سراب – بغداد

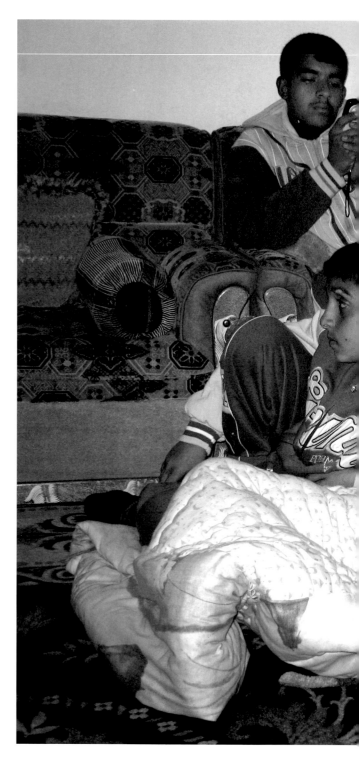

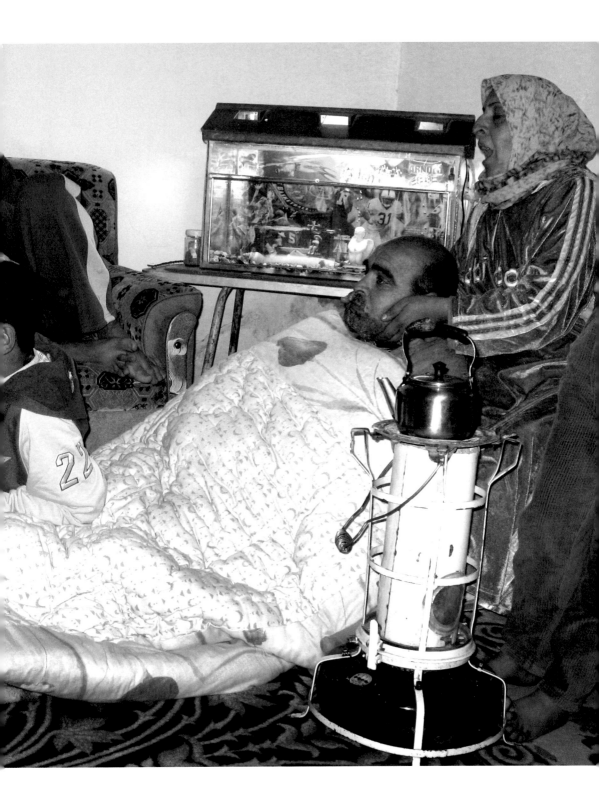

We now have to use a petrol stove to heat water. Jamil came into the room carrying a book – he tripped and boiling hot water spilled over him. His 9 year-old body was burned and scarred. Antoinette, Mosul

صار علينا ان نستخدم المدافئ النفطية لتسخين الماء كان جميل يدخل الغرفة حاملا كتبه عندما تعثر وانسكب عليه الماء الحار. احترق جسده ذا التسع سنوات وتشوه.

انطوانيت – الموصل

Previous page
I call my niece Hajir my small box of secrets. There are fewer girls in her class than there should be – sometimes parents are afraid and keep them at home. In other circumstances when life has become tough, or parents have been killed, girls are often expected to stay home to help raise the family. Women are a majority of the population in Iraq – what will our future look like if a lack of education marginalises these silent casualities? Sarab, Baghdad

الصفحة التالية
ادعو هاجر ابنة أخي الصغيرة.." صندوق اسراري الصغير ".. عدد زميلاتها في المدرسة قليل .. تخشى الاسر على بناتهن فيبقون عليهن في البيوت .. في احيان اخرى عندما تكون الظروف قاسية او يقتل احد الوالدين يتوقع من الفتيات البقاء في البيوت والقيام باعباء المنزل . في العراق تشكل الاناث اغلبية السكان . ترى اي مستقبل ينتظرنا إن غيب الجهل هذه الاغلبية الصامتة !! سراب بغداد

Angel is 85. She never married. She raised her brother's
children from when they were small. Recently she fell and
broke her hip but she may as well have lost her legs because
the operation she needs is no longer available. Cancer or
debilitating breakages are not a priority in these extreme
times. Angel's family have no time to take care of her and she
has been abandoned – she gazes into emptiness all day long.
Antoinette, Mosul

*February 14th, Valentine's Day, we send text messages to each
other on our mobiles. Instead of exchanging news of death and
destruction, we try to create a space where we can live our lives,
where we might be able to catch our breath.* Antoinette

أنجيل في الخامسة والثمانين، لم تتزوج يوما . ربت واهتمت بأبناء أخيها طوال عمرها ، كسر
حوضها وبحاجة الى عملية صار اجراء مثلها شبه مستحيل . في الاوقات الحرجة يعد علاج
امراض مثل السرطان او تلك التي تعيق حركة الجسم رفاهية . عائلة انجيل لاوقت لديها
للاعتناء بها . تمضي انجيل يومها وحيدة تحدق في الفراغ .. انطوانيت – الموصل

يوم 14 شباط .. تبادلنا المسجات على الموبايل .. هنئنا
بعضنا بعيد الحب .. نحاول أن نخلق فسحة من الحياة .. نلتقط أنفاسنا من تبادل أخبار
الموت والدمار .. انطوانيت

DESERTED

LUJANE, BAGHDAD

I used to stand on the steps of our house and cry while I watched my father putting his bags in the car. He was always travelling on business. Sometimes he took me with him. Other times, I was left waiting for his return. Every night, we used to sit around the TV and play dominoes till I fell asleep on his lap and he'd carry me to bed and tuck me in.

I really wanted to study medicine, but I had to study engineering. One of my schoolmates had much lower marks than me but she was the daughter of a Baathist, and could study what she wanted. I remember thinking "If my father was a Baathist, I could have studied medicine". I was angry and bitter. My bitterness deepened when my only surviving brother was arrested. He was legally exempted from military service, but a man wanting to extort money from my father tore up my brother's army record and my brother was imprisoned. We heard nothing for two weeks. Then one day when my mother went to visit him in jail she found him on the street on his way home. She collapsed. His clothes were torn and his beard had grown so long he looked like an Afghani fighter.

After university, I worked in a government office but I was unsatisfied and decided I needed change. I studied literature at night school. This time, my marks qualified me for what I wanted to do and I started my masters. My mother became ill and my nights were divided between studying and caring for her. Every night, I drank five or six cups of coffee to keep me awake. I got my degree and began teaching at university. I loved my work.

We started hearing that Iraq might be invaded. "We'll be worse off than the Palestinians" I said to my colleagues. They all laughed. But today, with all that's happening in the country, they're not laughing anymore.

One day, I came home from work and everyone was very upset. The dominant militia in our area had come to our house and threatened to kill us if we didn't leave the neighbourhood immediately; we were the 'wrong' sect. I stormed out of the house in a rage and went to their local headquarters. I tried to talk to them reasonably, I tried to use logic and in the end I felt I got the better of them. But, in fact, Iraq is not ruled by reason these days. Eventually they forced us out of our house. As Baghdad changed, so did my life. The streets of the city are empty of everything but destruction, concrete barriers and barbed wire.

DESERTED

I watch Baghdad everyday. I stand on our balcony: miles of terrible traffic jams, concrete barriers, checkpoints – dividing our city into a thousand pieces and delaying our journeys to work.

Every morning the sound of Fairouz singing on the radio battles with the car horns, ambulances, sirens and the blasts of explosions.

I'm a lecturer in a college. Normally, it would take an hour to get to work, but these days I arrive as the day is about to end. I try to use the time in the taxi reading. One day the Americans had closed a road, our driver turned around and took another route down a dirt side street. Suddenly there was heavy gunfire - someone trying to drive through a checkpoint. I sat watching, clutching my handbag in my lap. When I got home, I wanted to watch TV. I reached into my bag for my glasses. They were smashed and splintered. Rummaging around, I felt something cold and metallic: a bullet casing. I will never forget the terror I felt – that bullet could have gone through me.

I really miss my friend, Nahla, but I can't visit her anymore because she lives in Haifa Street and it's too dangerous to go there. There are always gun battles between sectarian militias and the National Guard. One day, a woman ran out onto her balcony to drag her generator into her flat so it wouldn't be hit and explode. She was shot and killed by a sniper. The woman left behind a 10 month-old baby. The story of the Haifa Street Sniper is a legend in Baghdad. I used to love walking down the street, but today, of course, like everyone in Baghdad, I change my route to avoid it. The only time I went near it, was to take my photographs. A group of kids shouted "Where do you think you're going? You're going to get killed!" National Guards stopped me, I tried to persuade them to let me through, but it was useless. They don't allow anyone onto the street but neither they nor the Americans do anything about the snipers.

I woke up when the phone rang. "I'll meet you in Bab Al Mu'adham", said my friend. Our house is in Salihiya and I had to take a safe route down the Muthana Airport Road and over Sarafiya Bridge. I took a cab, the road was absolutely jammed with traffic. Maybe a party leader, Member of Parliament or an American officer was passing, the roads were closed and everyone was forced to take a diversion via Sarafiya Bridge. I waited for almost 2 hours, then got fed up and decided to walk the rest of the way. I crossed the bridge…I remembered the seagulls picking at the bread people threw into the river. When I reached the other side, I saw the coffins of people killed by an explosion the day before.

Previous page
This might seem like yet another statue of Saddam Hussein, but they destroyed all the statues of him, one by one. And now they've destroyed Iraq and we're about to collapse altogether. This is the last statue left in Baghdad; Adnan Khairallah, the Minister of Defense during the Iran-Iraq war, is still standing in Shuhada' Square. Otherwise, it's empty. Shuhada' Square, Baghdad

الصفحة التالية
للوهلة الأولى، يبدو هذا تمثالا آخر لصدام حسين .. بدأ
الأمر بتدمير تماثيل صدام الكثيرة؛ واحدا تلو الآخر..
انتهى الأمر اليوم إلى تدمير العراق وكلنا نكاد ننهار..
هذا هو التمثال الأخير في بغداد – في ساحة الشهداء..
مازال عدنان خير الله، وزير الدفاع في الحرب العراقية
الإيرانية، واقفا في ساحة تخلو من أي شيء اخر ..
ساحة الشهداء – بغداد

Another empty street...Shuhada' Street.. I would walk here every Friday on my way to Al Mutanabbi Street, where I would meet my friends and buy books. ...But all this has ended. Now Fridays are curfew days. Shuhada' Street, Baghdad

شارع أخر خال، هو شارع الشهداء.. كنت أعبر هذا
الشارع للذهاب إلى شارع المتنبي لغرض شراء الكتب.
اعتدت أن التقي بصديقاتي وأصدقائي هناك.. كان
احتفالا ومزادا للكتب يقام كل جمعة. انتهى ذاك
الطقس اليوم، وصار يوم الجمعة حظرا للتجوال ..
شارع الشهداء – بغداد

This is Sheikh Ma'rouf Street, parallel to Haifa Street. It was always bustling but bit by bit, there were fewer and fewer people; less and less movement and life...as in all of Baghdad. Since the Haifa Street Sniper arrived, Sheikh Ma'rouf Street has completely emptied of people. Sheikh Ma'rouf Street, Baghdad

هذا شارع الشيخ معروف المحاذي لشارع حيفا.. اعتدت أن
أراه يعج بالمارة.. شيئا فشيئا، بدأ الناس يتناقصون والحركة
تقل.. مثله مثل بغداد.. لكن، ومنذ ظهور قناص شارع
حيفا، أغلقت المحال التجارية في الشيخ معروف وخلا تماما
من الناس ..شارع الشيخ معروف - بغداد

Next page
Al Umara' was the best restaurant and patisserie in Baghdad. It's in the Karrada area, which was relatively safe at the start of the occupation. My father used to love to buy us baklawa from there. Now, with all the bombings life has stopped. The Al Umara' restaurant & patisserie, Karrada, Baghdad

الصفحة السابقة
كان هذا أفضل مطعم ومحل للحلويات في بغداد...
يقع محل الأمراء في منطقة الكرادة؛ المنطقة التي كانت
تعد آمنة نسبيا في بداية ايام الاحتلال .. اعتاد والدي
ان يجلب لنا البقلاوة من الأمراء ..بعد العديد من
الانفجارات التي حدثت توقفت الحياة في المكان.
مطعم وحلويات الأمراء - الكرادة - بغداد

Haifa Street is mentioned in many
Iraqi songs, but today it is deserted:
just armed militias and units of the
National Guard firing at each other.
..even the palm trees are wilting.
Haifa Street, Baghdad

كان شارع حيفا يظهر في كثير من الأغاني العراقية
والعديد من الإعلانات .. اليوم الشارع خال، تتنازعه
مجموعات مسلحة وفرق الحرس الوطني... حتى نخيله
يذبل اليوم. شارع حيفا-بغداد

Next page
Shuhada' Bridge was one of my
favourite places in Baghdad...We used
to really enjoy watching people fishing,
spreading their nets, absorbed in their
work and singing their songs...seagulls
raced to pick up pieces of bread;
people would buy a hot loaf from a
nearby bakery, stand by the railings
of the bridge and throw crumbs into
the river...the fish...the seagulls.
But now, the bridge is closed.
Shuhada' Bridge, Baghdad

الصفحة السابقة
كان جسر الشهداء، أحد أماكني المفضلة في بغداد..
برغم قصر الجسر، كان المارة يستمتعون بمشاهدة صيادي
السمك وهم ينشرون شباكهم منهمكين بالعمل، يرددون
أغانيهم والنوارس تتسابق لالتقاط الخبز.. كان الناس
يبتاعون أرغفة خبز من مخبز قريب، يتوقفون عند سياج
الجسر ويرمونها إلى النهر .. الأسماك و النوارس. الجسر
اليوم مغلق.. جسر الشهداء - بغداد

This is a street in the Mualimeen neighbourhood in Bagouba. Armed groups control the whole city – they call it the Islamic Emirate. A lot of sectarian killings happen in this street. Innocent people are slaughtered in the Islamic way – "Halal butchery"!!!

Mualimeen, Bagouba (Diyala province)

هذا شارع في حي المعلمين – مدينة بعقوبة.. تسيطر الجماعات المسلحة على المدينة بأكملها، يسمونها إماراتهم الإسلامية ... كثير من أعمال القتل الطائفي تحدث في هذا الشارع، ويذبح الأبرياء على الطريقة الإسلامية (ذبح حلال). حي المعلمين، بعقوبة- محافظة ديالى

Next page
"For the good of Iraq, open your eyes". These adverts are repeated again and again on TV. They want Iraqis to inform on terrorists and anything that seems suspicious... The government spends millions of dollars on adverts like these, pasting them up on concrete barriers, in public squares and empty streets...

Concrete barriers, Baghdad

الصفحة السابقة
"لعيون العراق فتح عيونك".... تبث مثل هذه الإعلانات مرات ومرات يوميا، في محاولة لجعل العراقيين يبلغون عن الإرهابيين، وكل ما يمكن أن يثير الريبة والشك .. تنفق الحكومة ملايين الدولارات على مثل هذه الإعلانات وعلى لصقها على الحواجز الكونكريتية والساحات العامة، وعلى جدران شوارع تخلو من الناس.. حواجز كونكريتية – بغداد

المهجورة

أراقب بغداد يوميا.. أقف على شرفة شقتنا، ولا أرى سوى الزحام والاختناقات المرورية والحواجز الكونكريتية .. السيطرات ونقاط التفتيش تقسم بغدادنا الى الف جزء، تؤخر الجميع عن اعمالهم .

توقفنا عن سماع فيروز صباحا، واكتفينا بأصوات منبهات السيارات .. صفارات الإسعاف وسيارات الشرطة والحرس الوطني .. يرافق ذلك احيانا أصوات الانفجارات ..

أعمل مدرسة ف احدى الجامعات. الطر قُ تستغرق عادة ساعة.. وصلت مرات عدة إلى عمل وقد اوشك الدوام الانتهاء؛ إذ أكون يومها قد امضيت معظم النهار في السيارة، مستثمرة الوقت في القراءة . في إحدى المرات كان الأمريكان قد أغلقوا الطريق، سائقنا وآخرون غيروا طريقهم ليسلكوا آخر ترابيا . فجأة سمعت صوت إطلاق نار كثيف.. كان أحدهم قد حاول اجتياز حاجزهم الأمني.. لم افعل شيئا.. جلست أراقب وحقيبتي في حضني. مساء ،، وبعد أن عدت إلى المنزل، أردت مشاهدة التلفاز، حاولت اخراج النظارات من حقيبتي.. استغربت عندما وجدتها مهشمة.. أدخلت يدي في قاع الحقيبة. لامست أصابعي شيئا معدنيا باردا ..كان غلاف رصاصة. لن أنسى الرعب الذي اصابني حينها.. كان من الممكن ان تخترقني تلك الرصاصة بدلا من الحقيبة .

افتقد صديقتي نهلة... لم يعد بامكاني زيارتها فهي تسكن في شارع حيفا، هناك مجموعة مذهبية تسيطر على جزء منه، والحرس الوطني في حرب مستمرة معهم. في إحدى المعارك، ركضت إحدى النسوة إلى شرفتها، حاولت إدخال مولد الكهرباء لئلا ينفجر، قتلت برصاصة قناص، و تركت ورا ءها طفلا عمره عشرة اشهر.. تكاد حكاية قناص شارع حيفا أن تصبح أسطورة في بغداد .

كنت أحب المرور في هذا الشارع وانا ذاهبة الى العمل.. إلا أني اليوم، مثل كل البغداديين، غيرت طريقي لئلا امر عبره. المرة الوحيدة التي جرؤت فيها على الاقتراب من اطراف هذا الشارع، كنت أحاول التقاط صورا له.. صرخ في وجهي بعض الأطفال "أين تذهبين؟ ستقتلين". اقترب مني بعدها افراد من الحرس الوطني، حاولت إقناعهم السماح لي بالمرور، كان ذلك بلا جدوى. لم يسمحوا لي ولا لغيري من المواطنين، بالمرور. إلا أنهم والأمريكان الذين يملكون المنطقة لم يفعلوا شيئا ضد ذلك القناص.

استيقظت على صوت الهاتف؛ "ألقاك في باب المعظم" قالت صديقتي. بيتنا في الصالحية، وعلي المرور بطريق آمن عبر طريق مطار المثنى، ثم جسر الصرافية. استقليت سيارة أجرة، كانت الطريق شديدة الزحام، ربما كان أحد رؤساء الأحزاب، أو البرلمانين، أو الضباط الأمريكان، يمر في منطقة قريبة، أغلقوا تلك الشوارع بالطبع، وحولت، بالضرورة، جميع السيارات طريقها الى جسر الصرافية. انتظرت ما يقرب الساعتين في السيارة، قررت بعدها أن أتابع طريقي مشيا. عبرت الجسر.. مرت في ذاكرتي صور النوارس وهي تلتقط قطع الخبز، التي يرمي بها الناس إلى النهر من أعلى الجسر. عندما وصلت إلى الضفة الأخرى، شاهدت نعوش الاشخاص المقتولين في الانفجار، الذي وقع البارحة في هذه المنطقة ...

لجين – بغداد

كنت أقف على عتبة منزلنا وأبكي بينما والدي يضع حقائبه في السيارة...عمله يأخذه إلى أماكن مختلفة. كان يصطحبني مرات.. ومرات ابقى أنتظره. كنا نجلس مساءً حول التلفاز نلعب الدومينو حتى أنام في حضن والدي ... يأخذني بعدها إلى سريري ويغطيني .

أردت دائما أن أدرس الطب، لكني انتهيت لدراسة الهندسة.. أذكر زميلة لي في المدرسة درست ما تريد بالرغم من ان درجاتها الدراسية لم تكن تؤهلها لذلك .. لكنها كانت ابنة بعثي.. فكرت حينها "لو كان والدي بعثيا... لكنت منحت درجات إضافية

وحققت حلمي في دراسة الطب". غضبت وكان شيئا من المرار يكبر في قلبي.

ازداد مراري عندما اعتقل أخي الوحيد. كان قد سرح نظاميا من الخدمة العسكرية الإلزامية، احدهم أراد ابتزاز والدي لأخذ الأموال منه، اتلف ملف التجنيد الخاص بأخي وانتهى أخي إلى السجن. بعد أسبوعين من انقطاع اخباره خرجت امي لزيارته في سجنه لتتفاجئ به في الشارع عائدا الى المنزل .انهارت في وسط الشارع . كانت ملابسه ممزقة ولحيته قد طالت، بدا مثل المقاتلين الأفغان .

عملت في إحدى المؤسسات الحكومية لكني لم اكن اشعر بالرضا . قررت أن أغير اختصاصي، درست الآداب في إحدى الكليات المسائية. هذه المرة كانت درجاتي تؤهلني لأفعل ما أريد، بدأت بدراسة الماجستير.

مرضت والدتي وباتت ليالي موزعة بين الاعتناء بوالدتي ودراستي. كان على طاولتي دائما خمس أو ست فناجين قهوة علني لا أنام..

تعينت مدرسة في إحدى الجامعات.. كنت استيقظ منذ الصباح الباكر لأصل إلى عملي الذي اعشقه حد الجنون. بدأت تصريحات الأخبار تتناول احتمال غزو بغداد .. "سيصبح وضعنا أسوأ من الفلسطينيين".. قلت لزملائي في العمل.. ضحكوا حينها. اليوم ومع كل ما يحدث لم يعد اي منهم قادرا على الضحك .

عدت يوما من العمل لأجد الجميع حزاني.. زارتنا الميليشيا المسيطرة على حينا.. هددتنا وطلبت منا ترك منزلنا "لأننا من مذهب مختلف".. ثار غضبي وخرجت راكضة باتجاه مقرهم محاولة إيجاد مسؤولهم الذي لم يكن هناك حينها.. حاورتهم بلغة العقل والمنطق، شعرت باني تغلبت عليهم إلا أن المنطق لا يحكم عراقنا اليوم. تركنا منزلنا .

تغيرت حياتي كما تغيرت بغداد. شوارعها باتت فارغة إلا من الخراب والحواجز الكونكريتية والأسلاك الشائكة.

المهجورة

STRIPPED BARE

RAYA, BAGHDAD

As a small child, I lived in Algeria, and when my brother was born, I learned that babies actually come from their mother's womb and not from a stork in the high mountains, as my father had said. In my attic refuge I looked at clouds and drew what I imagined their shapes represented. I asked my mother what 'God' meant. She said He was the Giver. His first gift to me was the bicycle I'd wanted for so long.

We took a plane home to Iraq – but I was homesick for Algeria. In Baghdad, my Algerian accent made me a stranger. Every Friday, I walked around the city with my father and brother...from Shawaka we crossed the Tigris by boat to Souk Al Sarai and ended up in Mutanabbi Street. My parents taught me how to love Baghdad and I finally felt I belonged...

The Iran-Iraq war. In my classroom I heard the scream of air raid sirens. Mourning banners were hanging on all the walls and everyday there were processions, taking the dead to be buried. My father refused to admit all that was really wrong inside Iraq and I felt alienated from him. He was forced to join the Popular Army and sent to fight on the frontlines for many months.

I was desperate to go the College of Fine Arts, but my uncles said it wasn't a 'decent' place and my father refused. I went on hunger strike for three days - in the end, my father brought me the application forms himself. My friends and I dreamt of a time when there would be peace and we could set up our own studio in Rashid Street.

The Iran war ended in 1988 only to be replaced by the Gulf War in 1991. This time, my father conceded how corrupt the Ba'ath Party was. But he said " I am an Arab and Arabs don't abandon their comrades in times of trouble". My father was arrested in 1998, but Clinton was generous enough to bomb General Security headquarters and he was set free. "Our earth is bitter and produces only bitterness" he told my brother. "Leave". My father said he knew that the original values of the Ba'ath were destroyed the day they came to power, but he'd been too proud and stubborn to admit it. He kissed us goodbye and left the country.

We were crippled by sanctions and my friends and loved ones fled, leaving their keys with me. Maybe one day they'd come back to the city of the Tigris. I married and 'God the Giver' returned with my son, Bashar. But my husband and I had big problems and eventually I escaped by climbing out of a window, clutching my son in my arms...

April 9, 2003. The statue fell...'smart' bombs...'smart', but they killed our loved ones yet again. Hülagü has invaded our city in new guises - the beards of fundamentalist Islamists, the turbans of traitorous muftis and the masks of ugly thugs.

And 'God the Giver' has left, taking his bags. He's grown bored of our wars.

STRIPPED BARE

I just didn't feel like going to work and couldn't be bothered to get out of bed. I'm afraid every time I go out I'll hear we've lost another friend. I'm beginning to hate hearing the news...someone was killed, another lost his hand in an explosion...nothing but death and destruction.

I told work I'd be coming in late and sat down for a cup of coffee and chat with my mum. She began talking about how beautiful the weather was. That made me melancholic. For me, good weather is an invitation to walk around Baghdad's streets talking with my friends – Abu Nawas Street, Rashid Street, Mutanabbi Street - I drank my coffee in a hurry and smoked a cigarette that I didn't enjoy because all I was exhaling was pain and frustration. I went to work...a few hours later, a colleague ran into my office "They've assassinated Al Mutanabbi."

What did he mean? – The poet, Mutanabbi, died centuries ago. He said there had been an explosion on Al Mutanabbi Street. I screamed. "Has the Mongol leader, Hülagü come back? Have they sacked the city again? Will the river turn the colour of ink as it did when they threw all our books into it 800 years ago?"

Two days later I went with my friends to Al Mutanabbi Street to mourn another monument's collapse while we sit impotent, our hands tied, voices silenced and our will defeated by the weapons of war. I walked along the street looking for Abu Hossam and his bookshop, looking for the Shabandar Café and its clientele, looking for Adnan and his customers. Ash. Everywhere.

Alas, Mutanabbi. You were proud of your sword, and of your nights, and now they are breaking your mighty pen and quills – they are cutting out our tongues with a sharp sword and our nights are pitch black. I stand in the ruins of the Shabandar, the only remaining literary café in Baghdad. I am dazzled by the ash and blackness. Where did all the poets, writers, journalists, retired people, liberals, Communists and even Ba'athists go? Where are all the photographs of Baghdad in the 20's and 40's that used to line the walls?

During sanctions, poets, writers, intellectuals of all kinds, had to sell their books, on the pavements here, to feed their children. When the statue fell, we rushed to see if we could replace flimsy photocopies of books that we'd been forced to make, with proper bound volumes. I watch people's feet and I remember how my own feet grew year after year as I walked down this street. What an illusion to think that my son would also be able to grow up here. We stand mourning the ashes of the books, the destruction of the street and the bodies of our sons, which we can't even find. We didn't kiss them goodbye - they are not buried in the ground, but between the ashes of our books and our dreams – dreams that one day, our country will be well again.

He is a poet and when they asked him what he felt about
losing the place dearest to his heart, he responded by ripping
off his shirt and exposing his bare skin - a protest against sons
of this city who are ripping off its clothes and stripping it bare.
Al Mutanabbi Street, Baghdad

طلبوا منه، كونه شاعرا، أن يصف مشاعره حيال فقده أعز مكان على قلبه في بغداد، فما
كان منه إلا أن يظهر عريه احتجاجا منه على أبناء بغداد الذين يمزقون ثيابها ويخرجونها
لعريها مشوهة جريحة . شارع المتنبي - بغداد

Next page
My father used to walk all around Baghdad with me and my
brother. He introduced us to the great history of our country.
I wish that I could bequeath to my son what we inherited
from our father - but they have killed this dream. They
bombed Al Mutanabbi Street. Al Mutanabbi Street, Baghdad

الصفحة السابقة
كنت أسير دائما مع والدي وأخي الصغير في أرجاء بغداد يعرفنا على تاريخ وطن
عظيم. كنت أتمنى أن يرث ابني ما ورثته من أبي ولكنهم قتلوا الحلم داخلي.. فجروا
شارع المتنبي. شارع المتنبي - بغداد

Two days before the explosion, we were talking to Ahmed. Everything in his house had been stolen, including his 5000-book library. During sanctions we had to sell our books so we could live, but Ahmed preferred to starve. We suggested that he go to Al Mutanabbi Street – maybe the thief would try to sell his books there. But they were faster than we were; they burned Ahmed's books, Mutanabbi's books, Baghdad's books. Al Mutanabbi Street, Baghdad

قبل يومين من الانفجار، كنا نتحدث إلى صديقنا احمد، الذي سرق أثاث داره كله، ومعه مكتبته التي تضم خمسة الاف كتاب ، خلال سنوات الحصار، كنا نبيع كتبنا كي نأكل، لكن احمد فضّل أن يجوع على أن يبيع كتبه.. اقترحنا عليه أن يقف الجمعة في شارع المتنبي علّ السارق يحاول ببعها هناك، أو ربما نجد بعضا منها ..رحب بالفكرة. كانوا أسرع منا وأحرقوا كتب أحمد وكتب المتنبي وكتب بغداد. شارع المتنبي – بغداد

Previous page
The Tigris mourned Baghdad when the Mongol leader, Hülagü, invaded the city and threw all the books and manuscripts into the river – the water turned the colour of ink. Now Baghdad mourns its Tigris, which has become a hostage to barbed wire. Neighbourhoods have emptied – their residents forced to flee for their lives. And the sky has turned grey and black. We are lost – between the grieving mothers – in streets where once we loved each other like brothers. Al Mutanabbi Street, Baghdad

الصفحة التالية
أعلن دجلة حداده على بغداد يوم مر هولاكو ورمى بكنوزها من كتب ومخطوطات الى دجلة، وجعل لونه لون حبر مخطوطاتها.. وهاهي اليوم بغداد حزينة على دجلتها الأسير بالأسلاك الشائكة، وعلى أحياء هجّر أهلها... على سماء حال لونها إلى لون الرماد والسواد.. ضعنا بين أمهات ثكلى وبغداد تنوح أحياءها وشوارعها وأبناء لها، كانوا إخوة وأحبة. شارع المتنبي – بغداد

The Shabandar Café was the only literary place where we could still gather, the only café I could sit in without feeling I had to be ashamed of my female body; religion has named my pear breasts contemptible and the lavender between my thighs a disgrace. They were born from wombs just like mine, but they have abandoned God and his mercy.

Al Shabandar Café, Al Mutanabbi Street, Baghdad

كان مقهى الشاهبندر المقهى الأدبي الوحيد الذي يحتوينا جميعا....، انه المقهى الوحيد الذي أجلس داخله دون حرج من عورتي؛ أنا الأنثى التي أحال الدين كمثرتيّ المتدليتين في صدري، خزيا وجعلني أحمل الزنبق بين فخذي عارا.. ولدوا من ارحام تشبه رحمي لكنهم تخلوا عن رحمة الرب. مقهى الشاهبندر في شارع المتنبي – بغداد

This is the bookstore of Adnan Al Jabri, the "happy martyr"...
that's what was written on a black banner hung on the ruins
of his shop front...Adnan was proud that his shop was full
of books from the best publishing houses, but empty of
books written by people claiming to be sheikhs and Islamic
scholars. He refused to give in to their continuous threats
and now they have stolen his life and his history. Bookstore of
Adnan Al Jabri, Al Mutanabbi Street, Baghdad

كانت هذه مكتبة عدنان الجابري (الشهيد السعيد)؛ هذا ما كتب على قطعة سوداء
أمام أشلاء مكتبته..كان عدنان يفتخر بأن مكتبته هي الوحيدة التي تتواصل مع أفضل
المطابع، إلا أنها خلت من كتب لناس أدعوا أنهم علامة، وسيد، وشيخ، ومفتي،... رفض
تهديداتهم يوما بعد آخر وهاهم يفاجئوه بابتسامة صفراء،، فيسرقون عمره وتاريخه.
مكتبة عدنان الجابري / شارع المتنبي - بغداد

"Hush-a-bye, my little boy, sleep
Your enemy is sick
And far away, in the wild..."
My son has gone to sleep under the ashes and refused to
be separated from the books he loved, and the poets: Al
Sayab, who celebrated the rain, Zahawi who confronted
oppression, Rasafi, with his sarcasm, Jawahiri, who sang
the praises of the Tigris...
And here is my son sharing the wind with them – with no
grave and no headstone. Al Mutanabbi Street, Baghdad

دللول يلولد يا ابني دللول.. عدوك عليل وساكن الجول
نام ابني تحت الرماد ، وأبى أن نخرجه من بين قصائد أحبها ، السياب يوم غنى المطر ،
والزهاوي عندما رفض القهر، والرصافي بلسانه اللاذع ، والجواهري الذي أحب دجلة. وهاهو
ابني قُاسمهم الأثير دون قبر، دون اثر ، دون شاهد.. شارع المتنبي – بغداد

Next page
We stand here in silence, remembering the people we loved
now buried with the books and manuscripts. Here we are
standing where they left us; Adnan, Ghanim, Kutaiba,
Kadhim Mohammed Abu Hassan, Bilal, Bariq, Lu'ay, Bassem
and many, many others whose names we do not know.
Al Mutanabbi Street, Baghdad

الصفحة السابقة
نقف على الأطلال .. ، نستذكر ، بصمت ، أحياء دفنوا مع رماد كتب ومخطوطات.. وها
نحن نقف حيث غادرناهم.. عدنان ، وغانم ، وقتيبة ، وكاظم محمد أبو حسن ، وبلال ، وأياد ،
وبارق ، ولؤي ، وياسم... والعديد والعديد ممن لم نعرف لهم أسماء.. شارع المتنبي – بغداد

المسلوبة

تململت اليوم كثيرا في السرير، وتمنيت أن لا أصحو، وأبقى في فراشي أكثر.. مللت الخروج، وبت أخاف سماع خبر فقدان أحدهم.. بدأت أكره الأخبار: قتل فلان وفقد آخر يده بانفجار و.. كلها أخبار لا تحمل في ثناياها إلا الموت والدمار.. أخبرتهم في العمل، بأني سأذهب متأخرة هذا اليوم، وفضلت أن أشرب فنجان قهوة مع أمي ونثرثر.. بدأت أمي تتحدث عن روعة الجو هذه الأيام، وهنا بدأت الكآبة تتحفز للقفز الى روحي من جديد.. فالجو اللطيف بالنسبة لي، هو دعوة للمشي والتسامر مع الاصدقاء في أحد شوارع بغداد أو على دجلتها.. في شارع أبو نؤاس أوالرشيد أو المتنبي.

شربت قهوتي على عجالة، ودخنت سيكارة.. لم أستمتع بطعمها مع القهوة.. فالزفرات كانت تخرج منها ألما وحسرة.. ذهبت للعمل مشيا، علني أحقق جزءا من حلمي.. بعد ساعات من وصولي إلى العمل، دخل احد الزملاء ليخبرني أنهم اغتالوا المتنبي!!!!

ما الذي تقصده.. المتنبي مات منذ عصور.. من هو المتنبي هذه المرة؟؟. أخبرني أنهم قد فجروا شارع المتنبي!! صرخت فزعا.. هل عاد هولاكو من جديد؟!، هل سيحيلون النهر من جديد الى لون الحبر، بعد أن يرموا كل كنوزنا من كتب وتاريخ فيه.!؟.

بعد يومين، ذهبت مع صحبي ورفاقي إلى المتنبي لننعى صرحا آخر يتهالك، ونحن نجلس مكتوفي الايدي مخنوقي الاصوات مسلوبي الارادة امام آلات حرب عظيمة.

اسير في الشارع لأبحث عن أبي حسام ومكتبته.. عن مقهى الشاهبندر ورواده.. وعن عدنان والمحتفين بكتبه.. انه الرماد ..رماد في كل مكان.. مالك يا متنبي، وما للسيف لم قلت السيف والليل؟ هاهم يحيلون القرطاس والقلم لليل دامس، ويقطعون ألسنتنا بسيف جارح!

أمر على الوجوه .. أبحث عن وجه ضائع. يمر مقداد النقاش ويخبرني أنهم اغتالوا العلم والتاريخ لا البشر هذه المرة، ويقول لي: هاهو هولاكو يعود من جديد ليمحو تاريخ شعب وقصة حضارة.

أقف بين أعمدة الشاهبندر المقهى الأدبي الوحيد في بغداد.. أستغرب رماده وسواده، أين ذهب الشعراء، والأدباء، والصحفيون، والمتقاعدون، والليبراليون، والشيوعيون، وحتى البعثيون؟! أين صور بغداد العشرينيات والأربعينيات، التي تألقت يوما بعد آخر في جدران الشاهبندر!؟

ألم ينجينا هذا الشارع سنين الحصار العجاف، حين ملئت أرصفته كتب باحثي علم، وشعراء، وكتاب، وأدباء، ومثقفين، طال الفقر بطون أبنائهم فأفرغوا رفوف مكتباتهم/ كنوزهم الوحيدة وباعوها بالمزاد.. ويوم سقط الصنم، ركضنا إليه نحاول أن نستعيد أفراح كتبنا بأخرى طبعت بمطابع أنيقة، عوضا عن الكتب المستنسخة التي ملأت مكتباتنا.. بدأت أنظر إلى الأقدام، وتذكرت كيف كبرت خطواتي في هذا الشارع. كم كنت حالمة حين فكرت ان خطوات ابني ستكبر في هذا الشارع!

وقفنا على رماد كتب وخراب شارع، وجثث أبناء لم تطلها أيدينا.. لم نقبل جبينهم قبل وداعهم ونقل رفاتهم إلى تحت التراب، بل دفناهم بين رماد كتب وأحلام ..... أحلام بأن نصبح يوما ما على وطن.

ريا - بغداد

عشت في الجزائر.. وعندما ولد اخي أدركت أن الأولاد يولدون من رحم أمهاتهم، وليس كما اخبرني أبي ان اللقلق يجلبهم إلينا من الأعالي. بدأت أقضي ساعات أطول في صومعتي، أتطلع إلى الغيوم وأرسم بها ما أريد في مخيلتي. سألت والدتي يوما، عن معنى كلمة الله، فأخبرتني بأنه الواهب، وكانت هبته الأولى لي الدراجة التي تمنيتها.

عدنا الى العراق.. وفي الطائرة، شعرت بالحنين للجزائر.

داخل بغداد، كنت طفلة منعزلة تماما عن باقي الأطفال. أعيش وحدتي، كانت لكنتي الجزائرية تعني غربتي.

بدأت أسير مع والدي وأخي الصغير في أرجاء بغداد.. كانت لنا نزهة كل جمعة .. نذهب إلى الشواكة، ومن هناك نعبر دجلة بالبلم، ونزور سوق السراي ونختم جولتنا بشارع المتنبي.

اخيرا أصبح لي مكان انتمي اليه .. احببته من خلال أبي وأمي.. صار لي وطن..

في صفي المدرسي، سمعت صافرة الإنذار تعلن الحرب مع ايران.. أطلت علينا القطع السود، وعشرات الشهداء.. يزفون إلى قبورهم

بجروحهم وبزاتهم العسكرية، وزغاريد أم لم تكتمل فرحتها برؤية ابنها (عريس وربعة يزفونه) ..

كان والدي يرفض الحديث عن كل ما هو مشوه داخل العراق . ظل يكابر يوما بعد أخر. وكانت الهوة بيني وبينه تزداد عمقا . فارقنا

طويلا؛ حيث أمضى فترات طويلة في جبهات القتال، حين أجبر على الانضمام إلى الجيش الشعبي..

كنت أحلم بالانتساب إلى كلية الفنون الجميلة، رفض أبي بعد أن أخبره اخوته بأن الفنون هي ليست كلية للمحترمين. دخلت إضرابا عن الطعام لثلاثة أيام انتهى بخضوع والدي لطلبي و جلبه العديد من استمارات التقديم إلي، و ذهابه معي لاختبار القبول..كنت

واصدقائي نحلم بعراق آمن خال من الحرب، وأن يكون لكل واحد منا مشغل في شارع الرشيد.

تنتهي الحرب عام 88 ، لتبدأ أخرى عام 1991،حينها، اعترف أبي للمرة الأولى، بخراب البعث. وحين كنا نطالبه، أنا وأخي، بترك الحزب كان يقول لنا: (آني ابن العرب وابن العرب لا يترك صحبه ورفاقه وكت الشدة).

عام 1998 يعتقل أبي.. يمن علينا كلينتون بضربه موجهه إلى الأمن العامة؛ فيطلق سراح أبي، واعترف اخيرا لأخي: (يا المر.. كاعنا مرة ما تنبت إلا المر، اتركها).

يخبرني أبي عن سقوط قيم البعث في نظره منذ ثورة شباط ، يوم انتصر البعث، لكن أخذته العزة بالإثم.. وودعنا راحلا عن العراق ..

يهرب رفقتي وأحبتي إلى مدن، لا دجلة فيها ولا فرات، ويسلمونني مفاتيح أبوابهم علهم يعودون يوما.. وابقى ههنا، حارسهم الأمين.

أتزوج وأرى الله من جديد.. يمنحني ابني الوحيد بشار.

تتفاقم الخلافات مع زوجي، وأفتح نافذة منزلي لأفر منها، حاملة ابني الصغير بعد أن اقفل الباب علي..

2003-4-9 يسقط الصنم بقنابل ذكية.. وبالرغم من ذكائها، يسقط معها أبناء وأحبة من جديد.

يدخل علينا هولاكو بحلة جديدة.. بلحية إسلامي مكفر، أوعمامة مفتي غادر أومقنع بشع...

وغادرنا الله حاملا حقائبه بعد أن مل صراعاتنا..

المسلوبة

CAGED

LU'LU'A, KIRKUK

"I fell asleep for a moment...they were dressed in white with the faces of angels... they took you out of your cradle and carried you away... I was afraid. 'Where are you taking our child?' 'Don't be afraid, we are her guardians' they said 'we will always look after this lu'lu'a (pearl).'" My grandmother described the dream she had the day I was born.

My father was studying in Hungary and my mother was at work all the time. But my grandmother refused to have me raised by a nanny. She took me home with her when I was just 40 days old. My grandfather visited Turkey every year and from there he would drive to one of the European countries. I would sit next to him in the car as we drove to Austria...Greece...Yugoslavia. He used to buy me coloured pencils and kids' magazines in English and Turkish, my mother tongue. My grandfather started teaching me Arabic when I was four.

My grandmother died of cancer and I was left alone with my aunt and grandfather. When I was 13, my mother took me back to live with her. I went 'home' to my parents and my brother, and I felt like a stranger. My mother was my teacher in secondary school and I was terrified of her. It was she who chose that I would study veterinary medicine in university, which I wasn't interested in. We had to examine animals in their pens and when I came back, my friends would laugh at me. "Go away – you smell like a barnyard".

The sanctions were tough for everyone and the mood was dark. My aunt, who'd raised me, was like a real mother to me. She became ill and I used to rush home from college to feed and bathe her. When she died, I really lost something. I miss her. I was introduced to Mourad and one day, he asked me to marry him. I asked 'Why?' He smiled "Maybe I've started to love you". We got married two years after I graduated.

I opened my veterinary clinic. One week after we got married, my husband left me and went to Mosul to finish his degree. And once again, I was left alone – a stranger in an empty house.

I was watching TV with my mother-in-law. We cried when we saw Saddam's statue fall. We didn't like Saddam, not at all, but the scene was very ugly and I was angry that they didn't tell us about all the people who had been killed that day.

CAGED

Saturday, 10.10am, December 4, 2004. I was sitting in my clinic with Jamal, a trainee doctor. A client came to see us. He said he owned 800 sheep who needed treatment. Jamal and I got into a white pick-up with the man. He was dressed in a traditional Arab dishdasha. Ten minutes later, we were stopped by another pick-up. A man got out, pulled me out of the car, hit me. The client shouted to me. I felt guilty – maybe he was being kidnapped because of me.

They took us to a cave. They beat me on the head with a pistol butt and the walls started to swim. I felt the sting of rubber hoses on my skin; the client was whipping me! They drove us around the hills for hours. No signs of life. They dumped us into a hole in the ground, poured petrol all around and threatened to set it alight. "So be it – burn us if you're going to, but tell me why".

...They took Jamal away..."The phone rang and rang" he said, when they brought him back. "Your husband screamed when I told him what had happened and I could hear the whole house was in turmoil around him". After that, they took us into a mud room with no door. The creeping darkness scared me. Jamal was trembling with fear and cold. The whole time I just cried and recited the Koran. For the next 3 days I didn't sleep. They gave us dirty water to drink and I was never hungry. On the third day, they told me that my family had paid the ransom and they separated me from Jamal. He was crying "I'm afraid they'll hurt you if they separate us". In fact, the way they were looking at me scared me. I will never forget one man's face – his green eyes watching me with a kind of wild hunger.

"If you shout or look back at us, you'll die". I got out of the car and walked towards my husband's uncle who was waiting for me. A few blocks away, I saw my husband. He didn't hug me and his face terrified me..

"Did they rape you?" everyone asked – everyone but my husband. "No". Had the family's honour been preserved? Had I been raped? That's all that seemed to matter to them.

My husband left me to go on the Haj. All night, every night I cried bitterly.

I struggled to track down my kidnappers. One of them was arrested. A representative from his tribe offered me money to drop the charges. I was suffocating, but my family had borrowed $20,000 to free me and I had to pay it back. A few days later I signed the paper agreeing to drop charges, and I wept. I felt like I'd swallowed poison.

Months later I started to work as a journalist. I try to talk about my pain and the pain of others, I'm not allowed to go anywhere without my bodyguards. Every time we hear that a woman has been abducted, my husband stops talking to me for days. He's told me many times that I've destroyed his life...that I've shamed him.

Even though time has passed since I was kidnapped,
the memory of their ropes lives on in my wrists and the
threat of being beaten by their fists is no less present than
it was that day. They are always here. Violence is in my
every heartbeat. My relentless brain insists on calculating
the distance between me and the nearest gun, over and
over again. I try to keep my home full of beautiful things,
but the guns have invaded me and conquered. At home, Kirkuk

بالرغم من مرور زمن طويل على اختطافي، مازالت ذكرى الحبال على رسغي والخوف
من قبضاتهم وهي تضربني حاضرة وحية اكثر من ذلك اليوم . انهم دائما هنا معي .
الخوف من العنف يعيش مع كل نبضة من نبضات قلبي . يلح عقلي ولا ينوقف عن
قياس المسافة بيني وبين اقرب سلاح . حاولت ان ابقي على بيتي جذابا ورقيقا لكن
السلاح غزاه وتمكن منه . بيتي في كركوك

Next page
My mother says she is glad my grandparents are dead
and cannot suffer the shame of my kidnapping. She tells
my husband, "Keep her at home", "Don't let her work",
"Be careful what she wears, make sure she's covered
completely", "I don't want people to look at her", "I am
afraid for her". My husband has distanced himself from me.
I sit among them, I love them, but I am not really here.
At home, Kirkuk

الصفحة السابقة
تقول لي امي انها سعيدة لان جدي ميت ولا يعاني من عار اختطافي . تقول لزوجي "
ابقيها في البيت .. امنعها من العمل .. لاحظ ما ترتديه من ملابس واحرص على ان
تغطي كل جسمها .. لا اريد ان ينظر اليها الناس. . انا أخاف عليها " ابعد زوجي نفسه
عني . احبهم واجلس معهم لكني بعيدة عنهم . بيتي في كركوك

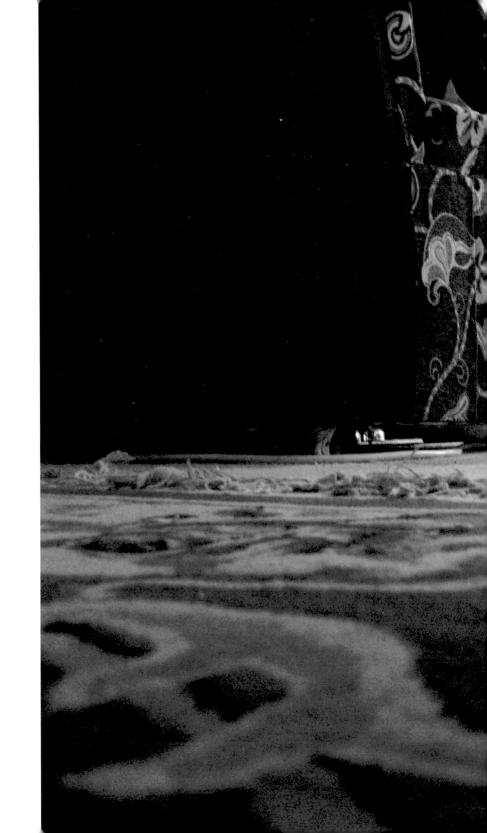

Since the kidnapping I haven't spent one day without my bodyguards. If I go to the market, they accompany me from shop to shop. When by chance I meet a friend...I stop to chat...but I lower my voice so they won't hear. In the car... the phone rings...I talk to my neighbour in a somewhat formal, unrevealing way. There isn't one detail of my life that these two bodyguards don't know. It leaves me wondering "How are they judging me?" At home, Kirkuk

منذ اختطافي لم امض يوما واحدا من دون حرس . أذهب إلى السوق، يتنقل حراسيُ الشخصيون ورائي من محل إلى آخر. أصادف صديقة.. أتوقف لأبادلها الأخبار، أخفض صوتي كي لا يسمعونا . أصعد إلى السيارة، يرن الهاتف، أحاور جارتي بشيء من الرسمية والغموض. ماعاد هناك تفصيل واحد في حياتي لا يعرفه هذان الحارسان. لطالما تساءلت عن الطريقة التي يحكمون بها على سلوكي. بيتي في كركوك

Previous pages
I felt alive when I used to watch the bustling street below. For months after I was kidnapped, I hardly looked out of the window at all...I'd make sure that my face was completely hidden behind the curtain. I would spend my days crying, reading the Koran and beating myself. At home, Kirkuk

الصفحة التالية
كنت اشعر اني حية وانا اراقب شارعنا المفعم بالحياة ، بعد اختطافي بقيت اشهرا عدة امضي الوقت بالبكاء وقراءة القران وضرب نفسي.. بالكاد أُشق النافذة.. أحرص أن وجهي مختف تماما خلف الستارة. بيتي في كركوك

Previous page

I open my eyes in the morning...I see the gun by my bed.
My husband and I go to sleep 'decent' these days. The threat
of an attack lies between us. Every night we talk less and
less before we sleep and we don't laugh together in the
morning anymore. At home, Kirkuk

الصفحة التالية

أفتح عيني صباحا .. أرى المسدس جنب سريري .
أنام وزوجي اليوم "محتشمين"، نخاف أن يهاجمنا أحد، بدأت المسافة بيني وبين زوجي
تزداد ، ما عدنا نتحدث قبل النوم، ولم نعد نضحك معا في الصباح. بيتي في كركوك

I'm growing tired of my fear...heavy...my husband's neglect.
I travel to forget...I pack my things and leave. I search for
a place where I can be free of my burden, but my world
follows me wherever I go. Weeks or months later I retreat
home...defeated...nothing new... At home, Kirkuk

تعبت من مخاوفي ومن همومي ومن تجاهل زوجي . اسافر لعلي أنسى .. احزم اشيائي
وأغادر . أبحث عن مكان اتحرر فيه من همومي غير ان عالمي يطاردني أينما ذهبت .بعد
أسابيع واشهر اعود الى بيتي مهزومة ... لاشيء جديد بيتي في كركوك

I used to go to these hills when I needed to breathe, to free myself of pent-up emotions and let off steam. That's where they drove me the day they abducted me. We drove for hours and hours until the landscape, so familiar to me, began to swim and I was completely disorientated. They put me in a hole and covered me in petrol. For three days, the smell didn't leave me. I remember everything I went through in that empty land...My body has healed, but I am left with a fear I can't get rid of...every time I pass here, my wounds are torn open again. Twoazkarmato, Kirkuk

كنت معتادة على الخروج الى هذه التلال كلما اردت التنفس والتحرر مما خزنته من هموم
..هذا هو المكان الذي اخذوني اليه بعد اختطافي . استمروا يقودون السيارة ساعات
وساعات حتى اضعت اتجاهنا تماما . وضعوني في حفرة وسكبوا البترول على جسدي
.. رائحة البترول لم تفارقني لثلاثة ايام . مازلت اتذكر كل مامررت به في تلك الأرض
الخلاء . تعافى جسدي لكني مازلت احمل خوفا لايمكنني التخلص منه . . كلما مررت
من هنا تنكئ جروحي من جديد . طوزخرماتو – كركوك

الحبيسة

السبت.. العاشرة وعشر دقائق صباحا.. 2004-12-4.. كنت جالسة في عيادتي مع جمال، الطبيب الذي كان يعمل متدربا عندي. أتانا مراجع، قال إنه يمتلك 800 رأس غنم يريد علاجها.. "تلقحين 400 اليوم وغدا الباقي" قال الرجل. غادرت العيادة معه ومع جمال لفحص القطيع، ركبنا سيارة بيك اب بيضاء، كان الرجل يرتدي الجلباب التقليدي الأبيض. بعد عشر دقائق أوقفتنا سيارة بك آب أخرى. فجأة اقترب شخص.. ضربني على رأسي.. صرخ في المراجع "حسابك بعدين".. شعرت بالذنب لحظتها.. ربما اختطف الرجل بسببي!!

اقتادونا إلى السيارة الأخرى، بعد نصف ساعة، أنزلونا في مكان ما.. ضربوني بعقب المسدس على رأسي وبدأت الدنيا تغيم. أحسست بعدها بلسع خراطيم مياه على جسدي، كان المراجع معهم يضربني!

أدخلونا إلى السيارة مرة أخرى، ظلت السيارة تدور في الصحراء لساعات.. لم أر أي معلم لحياة، من خوفي لم أشعر بالبرد، ولا بألم الرضوض التي تركوها على جسدي، توقفنا بعدها، رمونا في حفرة، سكبوا حولنا بنزين وهددوا بحرقنا أحياء.. "حسنا، فليكن، احرقونا ولكن أخبروني لماذا ؟!". تركونا في الحفرة ساعة، عادوا بعدها، واصطحبوا جمال معهم.. "رن الهاتف طويلا، أجاب زوجك، أخبرته.. صرخ.. أخبرته". وأحسست أن الدنيا حوله انقلبت رأسا على عقب" أخبرني جمال عندما أعادوه. ساقونا بعدها إلى غرفة طينية خربة بلا باب، كان الظلام الذي يزحف يزيد من خوفي، و كان جمال يرتجف من البرد والخوف. كنت أبكي وأقرأ القرآن طوال الوقت.

. لثلاثة أيام لم يغمض لي جفن، كان جمال ينام أحيانا. أعطونا مياه قذرة لنشربها ولم أشعر بالجوع أبدا. في اليوم الثالث أخبروني أن عائلتي قد دفعت المبلغ. كان يبكي "أخاف أن يؤذوك في حال فرقونا". كانت نظراتهم تخيفيني، لن أنسى أبدا ملامح أحدهم.. عيونه الخضراء التي تحدق فيّ بنهم. "

" إن صرخت أو التفت ستموتين". نزلت من السيارة ومشيت باتجاه السيارة التي كانت تنتظرني. كان خال زوجي ينتظرني، على بعد شوارع رأيت زوجي.. لم يحتضنني ونظرته هو الآخر أرعبتني، عندما وصلت البيت انهارت أمي. "هل اغتصبوك؟" سألني الجميع ما عدا زوجي، "لا" أجبت. كل ما عناهم حينها هو شرفهم، والشرف عندهم ينحصر بألا أغتصب.

غادرني زوجي ليحج، ولأشهر عشت عند أمي... كنت أبكي طوال الليل. بعد البحث والكثير من القلق وإحساس المرار، تمكنت من معرفتهم. قبض على أحدهم، جاءني ممثلون عن عشيرته عارضين عليّ إعادة المال مقابل التنازل عن حقي في مقاضاته.. بعد أيام وقعت وقعت ورقة التنازل. "لقد تجرعت السم ساعة وقعت" قلت لأمي.

بدأت الكتابة في الصحافة ، احاول التحدث عن المي والألم الآخرين.. لا يسمح لي اليوم بالذهاب إلى أي مكان من دون حارس شخصي.

كلما سمعنا أن أحداهن قد اختطفت، يتوقف زوجي عن محادثتي لأيام. قال لي مرارا أني حطمت حياته.. و أنني أخزيته.

لؤلؤة - كركوك

"غفوت لحظات.. رأيتهم بوجوه نورانية.. يرتدون البياض.. حملوك من مهدك.. خفت.. ناديت عليهم: إلى أين تأخذون ابنتنا الوحيدة؟.. التفتوا إلي.. قالوا لي بصوت واحد بعث في الطمأنينة: لا تخافي.. إننا حراسها.. سنحمي دائما هذه اللؤلؤة من كل شر" وصفت لي جدتي حلمها يوم ولدت .

درس والدي بهنغاريا، و كانت والدتي تعمل طوال الوقت. رفضت جدتي أن تربيني مربية، أخذتني وعمري وعمري أربعين يوما . كنت وخالتي أحضر حقيبتي الصغيرة، كان جدي يزور تركيا كل عام، من هناك يقود سيارته الى احدى الدول الأوربية. جلست إلى جانبه وذهبنا الى النمسا.. اليونان.. يوغسلافيا.. كان يشتري لي أقلام التلوين.. مجلات الأطفال باللغة الإنكليزية.. كنت أقضي أيام السفر أرسم أو اقرأ بالعربية أو التركية. بدأ جدي يعلمني العربية وأنا في الرابعة .. مرضت جدتي وتوفيت إثر اصابتها بالسرطان.. بقيت مع خالتي وجدي. في عمر الثالثة عشر، استرجعتني أمي. عدت لأعيش مع والديّ وأخي.. أحسست نفسي غريبة بينهم.. تابعت الدراسة، كانت والدتي هي مدرستي في الثانوية. كنت أخشاها. عند تخرجي من الثانوية ملأت أمي طلبات التقدم إلى الجامعة.. بدأت دراسة الطب البيطري.. فرع لم أرده.. كنا نضطر لزيارة حظائر الحيوان.. نتفحص أجزاءها. "ابتعدي.. رائحتك مثل رائحة الحيوانات" تضحك صديقاتي في السكن الجامعي ويطلبن مني الابتعاد عنهن.

عايشت الحصار.. كان قاسيا على الجميع.وكان مزاج الناس سوداويا .

مرضت خالتي، لقد ربتني كأنها أمي الحقيقية . كنت أعود من الكلية لأطعمها.. أحبها. عندما ماتت افتقدتها كثيرا.. كنت قد بدأت أتعرف إلى مراد. في يوم طلب مني الزواج.. عندما سألته لماذا.. أجاب ضاحكا "ربما.. بدأت احبك".. تزوجنا بعد تخرجي بعامين.

افتتحت عيادتي وبدأت العمل فيها.. بعد زواجي بأسبوع.. غادرني زوجي الى الموصل ليكمل دراسته العليا.. ومرة أخرى، بقيت غريبة في منزل فارغ.

كنت أزور حماتي.. بكينا عندما رأينا تمثال صدام يسقط.. لم نحب صدام يوما.. إلا أن المشهد بأسره كان شديد البشاعة.. غضبت لأنهم لم يخبرونا عن الضحايا الذين قتلوا اليوم!!

الحبيسة

FRIENDSHIP

DIMA (AGE 6), BAGHDAD

I love Iraq...I don't want to live anywhere else...No, I don't want to leave it... Everyone I love is here – my granny, my aunt, my uncle, all my family and friends... When I was very young and lived outside Iraq with my mum and dad, I didn't have any friends. My mum and I would stay in the flat all day long – yes, it's true my mum used to play and draw palm trees with me, but I didn't have any family there or friends...I was lonely...and my mum was lonely too.

I feel like Iraq is becoming empty...Everyone we know and love is going away and leaving us behind...like my friends – Nazaline and Aya and Hayat...A lot of my schoolmates miss classes. In my classroom, we used to have three rows of desks, ten in each row, and two of us sat at each desk. Now we only have 2 rows and there are just 5 girls in each row.

I love our area. It's the best neighbourhood in Baghdad. Nothing bad happens here...well, once a sniper shot a woman while she was walking past the generator in our street. My friend Nour's mother and brother saw him and told us. My aunt called my uncle to tell him not to come back that way and she and I took a different route to school that day. I told my aunt to call my mum. I was afraid she'd come back that way and the sniper would kill her too. But my aunt said 'your mum comes home a different way, anyway, so don't worry.'

If we have our own army, why are the Americans here? Why don't they kick the Americans out of our country? Anyway, don't the Americans have their own country? Why have they come here to ours?

Why are so many people dying here, when they're not sick or old?

One day Eugenie (sometimes I call her by a funny name but she doesn't get angry) asked me "do you want to take photographs?" I was really, really happy and I didn't let my mother use the camera anymore...I took pictures all the time...of myself, the house, the other girls in the project...I even took pictures of the toilets and bathroom and I took a picture of the tortoise in the house where we learned photography...she was called Tank Mother...it's not her real name...it's what we called her...

In Baghdad I love taking photos of my friends...My mum doesn't like me taking pictures of her...I really love taking pictures of people without them knowing... I love taking photos of myself a lot – I've taken so many pictures of myself... sometimes, I laugh and say 'it's amazing how much I like myself!'

FRIENDSHIP

Nour and Zeinab are my best friends now. When I get back from school, I do my homework and have my lunch quickly. Then they come over and we go out into the garden and play all sorts of games. When sunset comes, their mums or brothers come to take them home and my mum makes me go into the house...she never lets me stay in the garden. She always locks the door.

A few times, not many, my mum lets me sit on the bench in our street with my friends. She stands close by and sometimes my aunt or my grandmother sit by the garden gate and keep an eye on us. When I see a strange man pretending to be a beggar, I run and hide in the house and my friends run away to their houses too. He might steal us from our families and they would have to give him money to get us back, but probably he wouldn't give us back anyway, so we hide in our houses and he doesn't know there are kids here, and he gets tired and leaves. It's better that way, isn't it?

My mum takes me to school and back because there is no school bus. We registered 5 times, but all the buses stopped coming. The first driver was Aya and Tuqa's father – they were at school with me. He used to take us to school everyday, but then suddenly he stopped coming. Then Muhanad, my friend Nour's uncle, started driving us to school. He stopped coming too. The third driver just drove us home one day and that was that. The fourth bus was packed with children, we were like sardines, sitting one on top of the other – because there weren't enough school buses – but then that bus stopped coming too.

Note from Dima's mother:

Dima is six years old and my only child. I fear for her in school, in the street, at the gate of the house, and the garden. I always lock our gate and watch constantly from the window, in case one of the children manages to open it and run out into the street. A car might be passing and they might be kidnapped. It happens all the time.

I have to send Dima to school by bus, because walking is too dangerous, but the drivers are constantly being forced to leave. One fled his area because of sectarian pressure. The brother of another was kidnapped and killed and he left the country. Another simply disappeared and we don't know why. Dima's whole school life is unstable, with 4 changes of teacher in her current and first year. Sit Ibtesam was her favourite, but she left after an armed group invaded the playground and abducted the sweets kiosk owner. There was a gunfight in front of the gates, and a man passing by was killed in the crossfire. An hour later, the gang released their hostage, having kidnapped the 'wrong' person. Soon after, a bomb exploded in front of the guard's quarters. Parents became very frightened to send their children to the school, and Dima's class has now lost 60% of its students.

Nour and Farah at my house. They are
my neighbours...I played with them
everyday... but I can't play with Nour
anymore because after I took this photo
some people made her and her family
leave their house... My garden, Baghdad

نور وفرح ببيتنا... هن جيراني.. العب وياهن كل يوم
..بس بعد ما اكدر العب وية نور لان بعد ما اخذت
الصورة هذه الها أكو ناس جبروها هي وعائلتها حتى
يتركون بيتهم كراج بيتنا في بغداد

This is Abu Nizar's school bus. It's called the 'Squeeze and Crush' bus because Abu Nizar, the driver, arranges one on top of the other to fit us all in, as if we are sardines in a tin. These are my friends Zeinab, Siham and Fatima – my neighbours. Outside my school, Baghdad

هذا خط السايق ابو نزار . نسميه خط الجعيصة، لان السايق ابو نزار يسفط الاطفال واحد بحضن اللاخ مثل علبة السردين هذه صديقتي زينب.. سهام وفاطمة.. جيراننا .

صديقاتي في باص المدرسة- بغداد

Previous page
This is a picture of my friend Nour in front of Nazaline and Aya's house... they are not here anymore... I don't want to talk about sad things, I don't want to say whose house this is, or where they went or why. If I do, the picture won't be beautiful. My street,Baghdad

الصفحة التالية
نور صديقتي أمام بيت نازلين وآية.. تركو..ما أريد أحجي عن أشياء حزينة.. ما أريد أكول هذا بيت منو ووين راحوا وليش.. إذا كلت الصورة ما رح تكون حلوة.

شارعنا - بغداد

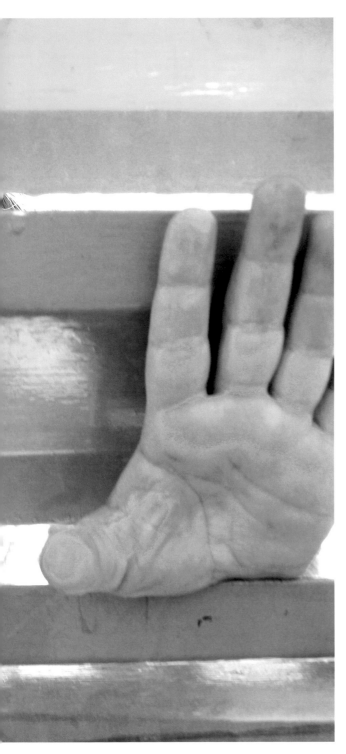

I am inside the house. These are my friend Nour's hands. She's in the street, on the other side of the garden gate shouting 'Dima, Dima' so I can let her in quickly. My house, Baghdad

إني بداخل البيت.. وهذه ايدين صديقتي نور.. نور ورا الباب تصيح "ديمة.. ديمة" حتى افتح الها الباب.
باب حديقة بيتنا في بغداد

Previous page
Farah is like an old man sitting on his chair and praying. My street, Baghdad

الصفحة التالية
فرح كاعدة على الدجة مثل العجوز اللي يصلي وهو بالكرسي. دكة جنب بيتنا في بغداد

Next page
Nour and Zeinab in our garden. They are my best friends. I love them a lot. My house, Baghdad

الصفحة السابقة
نور وزينب بحديقتنا. همة احسن صديقاتي. احبهم هواية
بيتي في بغداد

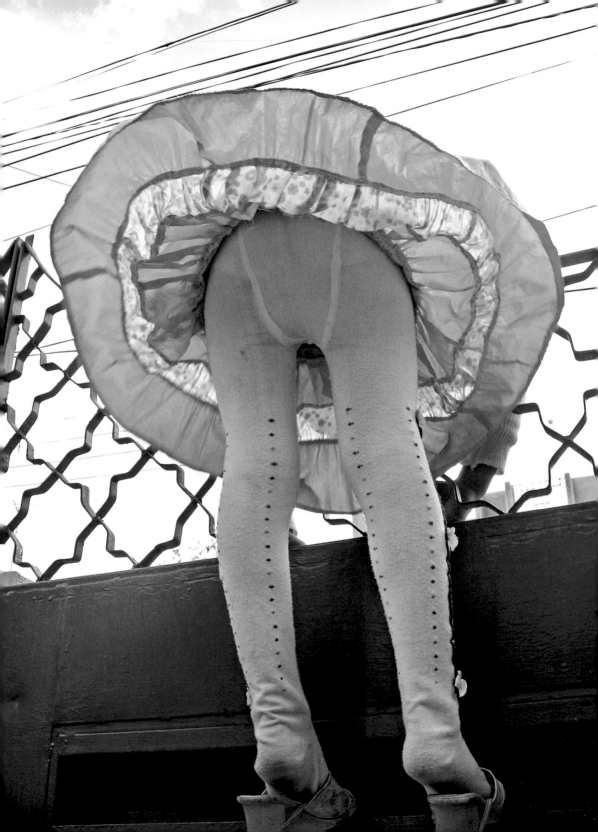

Nour's skirt blown up like a balloon in the wind.
My garden, Baghdad

تنورة نور المنفوخة مثل البالون. باب حديقة بيتنا في بغداد

Previous page
Nour climbing our garden wall – looking at the street.
I am in the street taking her picture. My street, Baghdad

الصفحة التالية
نور تباوع على الشارع.. هي صاعدة على سياج بيتنا.. آني أصورها من الشارع.
سياج بيتنا في بغداد

الصداقة

أهم شيء، بحياتي بعد ماما واسرتي، هو صديقاتي...نور وزينب هسة هن اكثر صديقاتي اللي احبهن . من أرجع من المدرسة أكتب واجباتي واتغدى بسرعة.. تجيني نور وزينب. نطلع بالحديقة ونلعب كلشي.. ولمن تروح الشمس ويصير الغروب، تجي أمهاتهن لو أخواتهن ويأخذونهن لبيوتهن، وأمي تدخلني بالبيت.. ما تقبل أبقى بالحديقة.. دائما تقفل الباب.. كم مرة.. مو هواي.. مرات قبلت امي اكعد على الدجة وية صديقاتي.. أمي توكف بمنا.. نوبات خالتي لو جدتي يخلن كرسي ويكعدن وراء الباب وينتبهن علينا.. لمن أشوف أي رجال غريب على أساس هو فقير اركض واختل بالبيت.. صديقاتي يفوتن ركض لبيوتهن ويختلن.. مو يجوز بيوكنا من أهلنا.. وأهلنا ينطونه فلوس.. يعني أمي لو خالي ينطوه فلوس وهماتين ما يرجعنا.. خو نختل ببيوتنا وما يشوف اكو اطفال ويتعب ويروح.. مو أحسن هيجي ؟

ماما توديني وترجعني من المدرسة لان ماعندي خط.

سجلنا بخمس خطوط لكن كلهم بطلوا.

أول خط مالت ابو اية وتقى، اللي هماتين وبايه بالمدرسة كان ياخذنا يوميا للمدرسة وبطل.

بعدين أخذنا خط مهند، اللي هو خال صديقتي نور، وهماتين بطل.

وعلى أبو الخط الثالث، وهذا ما اجه ولا مرة.. بس يوم واحد رجعنا من المدرسة وبعدين بطل.

الخط الرابع جان مليان اطفال لان ماكو باصات تودينا للمدرسة .. نسميه خط "الجعيصة " بس هذا همينة بطل أنا أم ديمة. عمر ديمة ست سنوات وهي طفلتي الوحيدة. أخشى عليها وهي في المدرسة، وهي في الشارع، وعند بوابة المنزل، حتى في حديقتنا. أحرص دائما على إقفال بوابة الحديقة وعلى مراقبة طفلتي من النافذة.. خوفا من أن تتمكن إحدى البنات من فتحها والخروج إلى الشارع، من السهل أن تمر سيارة وتختطفهن. يحدث هذا الأمر في عراقنا طوال الوقت.

مدرسة ديمة قريبة، لكن السير خطر جدا ..مضطرة لإرسالها في باص .. و سواق الباصات يجبرون دائما على الرحيل لسبب أو لآخر. أحدهم اضطر لأن يهرب من حيه من لأسباب طائفية .. أما الثاني فقد خطفت أحدى الميليشيات أخاه وقتلته، فهرب خارج البلاد . الثالث ببساطة اختفى ولا نعرف لماذا!!

حياة ديمة المدرسية غير مستقرة.. تغيرت أربع معلمات لها في سنتها الأولى والحالية من الدراسة.

ست ابتسام كانت المفضلة لديها وقد أحبتها فعلا. في إحدى الأيام هاجمت إحدى المجموعات المسلحة المدرسة مطلقة النار، نشبت معركة عند بوابة المدرسة، قتل بائع غاز كان يمر بالمصادفة، اختطفوا صاحب الحانوت في المدرسة. علمنا بإطلاق سراحه بعد ساعة، لأنهم اكتشفوا بأنهم اختطفوا الشخص الخطأ.. لكنه لم يعاود القدوم الى المدرسة بعد ذلك . بعدها بوقت قصير، فجر احدهم قنبلة في غرفة حارس المدرسة. خاف الأهل بعدها من إرسال أطفالهم إلى المدرسة وخسر صف ديمة 60% من طلابه.

ديمة – بغداد

آني أحب العراق.. ما أريد أعيش بعيدة عنه.. إي ما أريد اتركه.. بيه كل اللي أحبهم.. جدتي.. خالتي وخالي وكل اهلي وصديقاتي.. لمن كنت عايشة ويه أمي وأبوي خارج العراق واني اصغيرة كلش .. ماكان عندي صديقات.. أني وأمي كاعدات طول اليوم بالشقة.. صحيح أمي جانت ترسم وياية النخل وتلعب.. بس ماجان عندي اهل ولا صديقات.. جنت وحيدة.. وأمي هماتين جانت وحيدة..

أحس العراق بدأ يفرغ.. كل اللي نعرفهم ونحبهم صاروا يتركونا ويروحون.. صديقاتي: نازلين وأية وحياة.. هواي من صديقاتي بالمدرسة صارن يغبن وميجن للدوام.. صفنا جان ثلاث سراوات وكل سره بيه عشر رحلات.. وكل رحلة بيها اثنين. هسة صار عدنا بس سراوين وكل سرة بيه خمسة طالبات بس.

أحب منطقتنا كلش هواي .. هي احسن منطقة ببغداد .. كلشي ما صار بيها .. يعني بس مرة اكو فد قناص كتل وحدة جانت مارة من يم المولدة مال شارعنا . ام نور صديقتي شافت الحادث وكالت النا . اتصلت خالتي بخالي وكالتله، حتى لا يمر من ذاك الطريق . وهي بذاك اليوم اخذتني للمدرسة من غير طريق . طلبت من خالتي تتصل بامي جنت خايفة تمر من هناك ويموتها القناص . بس خالتي كالت لاتخافين امج ماتجي من ذاك الطريق .

إذا عدنا جيش ليش اكو أمريكان . ليش ما يطردون الأمريكان من بلدنا ؟ بعدين الأمريكان مو عدهم بلد.. ليش جايين لبلدنا ؟؟

ليش الناس يموتون ببلدنا وهمه مو مريضين لو عجوزين؟

فد يوم بوجيني (نويات اسمها عوجيني بس هي ماتزعل مني) سألتني تريدين تصورين؟ اني فرحت هواي وماخليت امي تستخدم الكاميرا . صورت طول الوكت .. صورت نفسي .. البيت .. البنات اللي بالمشروع .. حتى الحمام صورته وصورت السلحفاة اللي بالبيت اللي درسنا بيه التصوير .. اسمها (ام درع) هذا مو اسمها الحقيقي بس احنا سميناها . ببغداد احب اصور صديقاتي .. أمي ماتحب اصورها .. أحب اصور الناس بدون ما يدرون .. أحب اصور نفسي كلش هواي .. نويات اضحك وأكول " اني اشكد معجبة بنفسي ؟ "

الصداقة

DETACHED

SARAB, BAGHDAD

My mother sold all her jewellery to pay for a house for us. She worked day and night, carrying the bricks to the builders with her own hands.

We grew up...and she cared for us...we were happy in that house. But suddenly, with no warning, my father decided to sell it, and that's when our problems started. "It's my house and I can do what I want". He left us.

My mother got ill. The arrest of my brothers in 1995 was the final straw for her; 'I need to see them again so I can die in peace". But she only managed to see my brothers in prison a few times. Her health got worse and worse till she stopped being able to speak. She communicated with signs and gestures.

I remember the sound of the phone ringing. I raced home to find my mother's coffin in the middle of the room, surrounded by candles. There was a light rain and the calm chanting of the Koran – it stilled my heart. It was the first death I'd ever seen.

I felt I was losing everything I loved.

I tried to keep her dream alive, I didn't want to lose her twice so I finished university and got my degree. My two sisters left to get married but I stayed – alone with my old father in a small, suffocating flat – made even tighter by my father's rejection of me, and his anger whenever he thought I might marry and leave him. He was old and senile and said terrible things about my mother.

I went to work and I tried to dream again. We moved in with my brother and his family.

"Baghdad Airport is now under the control of the American forces": We were all sitting on the steps, listening to the radio. I cried. I felt I was losing my house and my mother all over again. 'How could Baghdad have fallen so easily?'

My father died just months later. I was relieved. I was sad.

I carried on going to work. One day I went to get my new ID papers from a government office. I was searched and let into the building. Moments later, a car bomb exploded nearby. I remember the smell of blood, people screaming, and running. I found shards of shrapnel in my headscarf.

DETACHED

One year and five months after the occupation began, the company I worked for went downhill. They didn't get any more contracts and work stopped, so finally I left.

I started watching people through my window. I noticed a shocking thing: everyone who walked by looked nervously over their shoulder – terrified, expecting a sniper's bullet or a mortar attack. And sometimes, days went by and I saw no one in the street. Where are the people? Why don't I see anybody? Are they just like me, scared to leave their houses?

I hide in my room and try to block out the non-stop sound of bombs. I try to escape by sleeping but the damned sound keeps waking me up. There is no escape anymore. I go to sit with my brother's family and all I hear is "an explosion happened here or there and so many people have died..." I don't want to hear about death or explosions anymore, I am forced to retreat to my room.

My little niece, Hajir, kills time with me. She comes into my room and she listens. I talk about everything, not caring about whether, being so young, she can really understand what I'm saying. One day she'll leave me too – to get married or to study – to live her life.

My sewing machine helps me to survive my loneliness. I work on it and feel some kind of achievement: a dress for a child, or a curtain for a neighbour. I can communicate better with my sewing machine than with people.

Every time I try to break my isolation and leave the house, something happens which forces me back home. Once I went to visit my sister. A few moments after leaving her house, a car bomb exploded nearby. I didn't know where I was – people screaming, smoke everywhere...my phone was ringing, but I couldn't even move my hand to answer it. Suddenly I saw my sister running towards me in terror, barefoot. All I wanted to do was to get away. I was very afraid the explosion would be followed by another one. I ran into my room. I tried to silence the noise in my head, but it wouldn't go away. I couldn't sleep for days.

Once again I tried – I went back to work. One day on my way in, I saw a man lying on the ground covered in bloodstained newspapers. It was at the Baya' bus station. I hurried past – I'd never seen a murdered person before. I took a taxi to the Bab al Mu'adham area. I was distracted, scared and confused – people walk past a dead body on the street and they don't even seem to notice. Murders are too ordinary in Iraq these days.

I wake up in the morning and the first
thing I see is this airship. It's one of
four that watch Baghdad day and night.
I want to hide and watch this thing that
is watching us all the time. I do wonder
how it is, that with all this technology,
they don't manage to limit the violence
cursing our lives. All the way up there,
are they just watching the victims?

The view from my window, west Baghdad

الصفحة التالية
أستيقظ صباحا، وأول ما تقع عليه أنظاري هو هذا المنطاد .
إنه واحد من أربعة مناطيد تراقب نهارات وليالي بغداد ..
اشعر برغبة لمراقبة ذاك الذي يراقب حياتنا، و أتساءل دائما
"كيف لم يتمكنوا، بكل ما يملكون من أجهزة مراقبة، من
الحد من أعمال العنف التي تحصد أرواحنا.. هل يراقبون
الضحايا فحسب؟ مشهد من نافذتي – غرب بغداد

I watch my street through a crack in
the gate. Even if somebody passes,
I only catch a fleeting glimpse of their
shadow to remind me there is a world
beyond my garden wall – a world that
my fear detaches me from.

Sitting at my window, west Baghdad

أراقب الشارع من خلال فتحة في الباب .. لاأكاد ارى
من المارة غير ظلهم الخاطف وهو يذكرني ان هناك ماهو
خارج جدران حديقتي .. عالم أبعدني الخوف عنه .

عبر نافذتي – غرب بغداد

I put on my coat and go into the garden,
willing myself to open the gate and go
out and not to think about the blood-
soaked newspaper on the pavement,
covering the murdered man's face. And
I find myself back in that dark basement
flat with my father all those years ago.

My garden wall, west Baghdad

ارتدي معطفي وأخرج الى الحديقة .. اجبر نفسي على فتح
الباب والخروج الى الشارع وان لا افكر بالجريدة المنقوعة
بالدماء وهي تغطي وجه رجل مقتول على قارعة الطريق
لكني أجدني عالقة في قبو مع والدي طوال سنوات مضت .

جدار حديقتي – غرب بغداد

Next page

I fill my solitude with fantasies of what
might have been – all the possible
scenarios unfolding around certain
times in my life – the husband I would
have loved and cared for, our lives
cradled in the walls of the house my
father sold from under us. I dream I am
sitting by its garden gate waiting for my
children to come home from school.

The view from my window, west Baghdad

الصفحة السابقة

أشغل عزلتي بخيالات حول ما كان يمكن أن يحدث من
حولي في أوقات محددة من حياتي : الزوج الذي أحب
والأعتناء به .. حياتنا المتأرجحة بين جدران بيت باعه
والدي من دون ان نعرف . احلم بالوقوف بباب الحديقة
بانتظار اطفالي وهم يعودون من المدرسة .

مشهد من نافذتي – غرب بغداد

Previous page left

I so want to know the world, but the
streets are all explosions, mud and
sewage. They stopped maintaining the
roads a while ago. The workers are
frightened of being killed. The never-
ending bombs are destroying what has
already been destroyed. I'd rather stay
home. Outside my door, west Baghdad

الصفحة التالية

أرغب بالتعرف على العالم... ولكن، أنى لي الخروج إلى
شوارع تملؤها الانفجارات والأوحال وطفح المجاري.. لقد
توقفوا عن صيانة الشوارع منذ زمن، يخشى العمال أن
يقتلوا.. الانفجارات المتكررة تزيد من خراب هذه الشوارع.
أفضل البقاء في منزلي. عبر الباب -غرب بغداد

Previous page right

My brother's family took me and my
father in when I couldn't look after him
on my own anymore. They are kind to
me. As I wash the rice, I imagine that I
am inviting them for lunch in my own
house, with my husband and children.
At home in Baghdad

الصفحة التالية

اخذني اخي واسرته عندما لم أتمكن من الأستمرار بالعناية
بوالدي لوحدي . يعاملونني بطيبة. بينما اغسل الرز ،
اتخيل اني ادعوهم لتناول الغداء في بيتي مع زوجي
واطفالي . . .في بيتى ببغداد

I spend long hours at my sewing
machine. The immediate world around
me disappears. The electricity cuts and
I'm back in the darkness of my room.
My sewing machine is as lifeless as I am.
At home in Baghdad

أمضي ساعات طوال امام ماكنة الخياطة،
يختفي العالم من حولي، وتنقطع الكهرباء، فأعود الى ظلمة
غرفتي. ماكنتي جامدة بلا حياة مثلي.
في البيت، بغداد

I run into my bedroom, hoping to calm my fear. Awakened by gunfire and mortars, I'm denied even the quiet refuge of sleep. The view from my window at night, west Baghdad

اهرب إلى فراشي عسى أن تفارقني مخاوفي . توقظني أصوات الإطلاقات النارية والهاونات.. لم يعد حتى النوم مهربا ..مشهد من نافذتي ليلا – غرب بغداد

العزلة

بعد سنة وخمسة اشهر من الاحتلال، ساءت أعمال الشركة التي كنت أعمل فيها، توقفت العقود وتوقف العمل.. تركت عملي ...بدأت أراقب الناس من خلال النافذة . كان المارة يتلفتون خلفهم خوفا من طلقة قناص او قذيفة هاون. أحيانا تمر أيام طوال لا اري فيها احدا في الشارع ولا يمكنني إلا أن أتساءل: أين هم الناس.. لم لا أرى أحدا؟؟ هل يخافون مثلي الخروج من بيوتهم؟

اقفل الأبواب ليس خوفا علي فقط بل علي أخي وأسرته، التجأ إلى غرفتي وأحاول نسيان أصوات الانفجارات التي لا تهدأ.. أحاول النوم.. توقظني تلك الاصوات اللعينة.. ما عاد من مهرب.. أذهب للجلوس مع اسرة أخي.. كل ما اسمعه هو"حدث انفجار هنا أو هناك.. مات العديد من الأشخاص"..

لا أريد أن اسمع عن الموت والانفجارات وقصص الاختطافات.. أعود مجبرة إلى غرفتي..

ابنة أخي الصغيرة "هاجر"، تقتل بعضا من موات الوقت، تأتي إلى غرفتي وأحدثها.. بكل شيء أحدثها وأحدثها.. أبوح لها من دون ان ابالي إن كانت قادرة على فهم حكاياتي وهي في هذا السن.. انها صندوق أسراري الصغير.. إلا أن هذا الصندوق ليس ملكي. سيأتي اليوم الذي تتركني فيه لتكمل دراستها.. تتزوج.. تعيش حياتها.

ماكينة الخياطة تعينني احيانا أخرى.. اعمل عليها.. علي اشعر بانجاز ما: فستان طفلة او ستائر لأحد الجيران. أشعر أني أتواصل معها أفضل من العديد من الأشخاص.

كل مرة احاول فيها كسر عزلتي والخروج من المنزل، يحدث أمر يعيدني إلى غرفتي. حاولت مرة زيارة اختي، وبعد مغادرة منزلها بلحظات انفجرت سيارة مفخخة بالقرب مني. أحسست حينها أني فقدت إحساسي بالمكان. كان الدخان يغطي كل شيء، و صراخ الناس يصم الآذان...كان هاتفي يرن.. لم أتمكن حينها من تحريك يدي للرد. فجأة رأيت أختي تركض باتجاهي حافية مرتعبة. كل ما أردته حينها هو الابتعاد خوفا من ان يتبع الانفجار بآخر. دخلت غرفتي محاولة إسكات الأصوات، إلا أن الأصوات لازمتني أياما ومنعتني من النوم.

حاولت مرة أخرى،وهذه المرة، عدت إلى العمل. في طريقي الى العمل يوميا وفي گراج (الباعة)، شاهدت رجلا ممدا على الارض مغطى بصحف مبللة بالدم. كنت أسير بسرعة قريبا منه، لم أكن قد رأيت من قبل شخصا مقتولا عن قرب. استقليت سيارة اجرة إلى باب المعظم وكنت مشتتة الافكار، مرتعبة، وحائرة وأنا أرى الناس يمرون بالجثة ويواصلون طريقهم دون اكتراث.. بات القتل مألوفا في العراق.

سراب - بغداد

باعت أمي مجوهراتها لتبني منزلنا.. عملت ليل نهار.. ساعدت العمال.. تقرحت يداها من حمل الطابوق .
كبرنا واعتنت بنا، كنا سعداء بذلك المنزل. فوجئنا عندما قرر والدي بيع البيت، وبدأت المشاكل بالازدياد ، وتركنا والدي قائلا "بيتي وانا حر .. افعل ما أشاء".

مرضت أمي .كان قراري بالعمل نافذة أمل فتحت في حياتي من جديد، حاولت، عبرها، التخلص من آلام وجروح تركتها حروب متتالية سحقت الجميع؛ بمن فيهم اسرتي .

لقد كسر اعتقال أخوتي عام 1995 أمي، ازداد مرضها حتى عجزت عن الكلام، كانت تتواصل معنا بالاشارات "أراهم.. عندها أموت بسلام" تمنت والدتي. بعد بضع زيارات لأخوتي، ماتت أمي بصمت فأغلقت نافذتي من جديد.

اذكر رنين الهاتف .. أسرعت في العودة الى المنزل لأجد كفنها يتوسط الغرفة محاطا بالشموع.. كان المطر خفيف وصوت ترتيل القران هدئ من روعي قليلا.. كان ذلك الكفن الاول الذي رأيته في حياتي ...

شعرت باني افقد كل ما احب ..

حاولت الابقاء على حلمها علي لا أخسرها مرتين ...

أكملت دراستي الجامعية وحصلت على الشهادة، الا أن والدي أغلق النافذة التي ما كادت تفتح.. تركتني أختاي ليتزوجن، وبقيت وحيدة مع والدي العجوز في منزل صغير خانق، ضاق المنزل أكثر برفض والدي وغضبه من فكرة زواجي واحتمال تركي اياه وحيدا. كان عجوز يخرف، وأحيانا يقول أشياء سيئة عن والدتي. بالنهاية كلانا انتقل الى منزل أخي.. أحكم إغلاق النافذة وعدت إلى وحدتي ..

واصلت عملي في الشركة، كنت أحاول أن احلم من جديد.

" مطار بغداد في يد القوات الأمريكية" ردد صوت المذياع.. كنا نجلس على السلم. بكيت. شعرت وكأني فقدت منزلي وامي ثانية، كنت أتساءل: كيف تسقط بغداد بهذه السهولة!!

ساءت الأوضاع يوما بعد أخر.. توفي والدي بعد سقوط بغداد بأشهر، ارتحت وحزنت ..

واصلت الذهاب الى العمل. وفي يوم ذهبت لجلب هويتي الجديدة من مؤسسة حكومية. تم تفتيشي ودخلت المبنى .. بعد لحظات انفجرت سيارة قرب المكان.. اذكر رائحة الدم وصراخ الناس وهم يركضون.. كانت شظايا صغيرة تملأ حجابي.

العزلة

MOTHERHOOD

ANTOINETTE, MOSUL

When my sister married the house was full of celebration, but when I asked my mother to reduce my household chores so I could study and go to university she said "Do you think going to university is any way for a girl to provide for her family?"

So, I started working and was happy. One day, I came home to find the parents of my brother's friend asking for my hand in marriage and I was engaged to Nidhal. He was doing his military service. The war with Iran had just started so I wasn't able to see him for a long time. I felt like I didn't know him at all and wanted to end my engagement. I spoke to my father. "Don't even think about it" he said "I will kill you, it is out of the question for our girls to do something like that."

Two and a half years passed. When we realised the war wasn't going to end any time soon, we decided to get married. My husband could only spend a week with me after the wedding before he had to go back to his barracks in Mosul. In the first 6 months of our marriage, I saw him 3 times. I resigned from my job and followed him there where I could, at least, see him once a week. 2 years later our daughter Sara was born.

I was watching TV - they said the war had ended and I literally leapt for joy, forgetting for a moment that I was pregnant. My husband finally came home to me and we lived together for the first time. In 1991, they stole him again when the Gulf War started. People said that Saddam would attack Israel, and the Americans would go crazy and bomb us with chemical weapons. We put white tape over our windows so the glass wouldn't shatter, we stockpiled water and put together first aid kits. I stuffed gauze strips with cotton and coal to use as protection against chemical attack. Our nightmares didn't come true, but, still, the sky was filled with dense black smoke – fires, explosions and black rain...I gave birth to my son. He wasn't fair like his siblings, and we laughed: "Maybe the smoke darkened his skin".

The sanctions were hard. We had to sell everything to eat; my gold jewellery, our furniture and clothes. The kids were growing up and I registered at university. I felt that at last I could realise my old dream. I used to walk to college clutching my books, with my daughter at my side on her way to high school.

April 9, 2003 – We sat watching TV in my husband's family's house. They were tearing down Saddam's statue. I cried silently. I looked at my 3 children. Their faces were sad. "Are you really crying for Saddam?" my sister-in-law asked angrily. "On the contrary, I am crying for the destruction that our country will inevitably suffer".

MOTHERHOOD

My daughter, Sara, and I ran to the kitchen window to see what was happening. Three American tanks lumbered down our narrow street, tearing up the trees by their roots. They stopped in front of our house. I was terrified. I looked at Sara. Maybe they'd stopped because they were annoyed we were watching them. Missiles had been launched from our neighbourhood the day before and they were searching the area.

They kicked our door again and again. I forbade my children to go anywhere near it. My husband let them in. They sprawled on the living room couches. My three children and I sat together on one sofa. I was trembling.

"Are you Christian?" They must have noticed the cross hanging on the wall.

"Yes" my husband answered.

"Do you support our presence here?"

"No...you've brought nothing but fire and destruction"

"So, you love Saddam, then?"

"Of course not, he burned the best years of our lives and he brought you here, didn't he?"

"And the present government?"

"They've achieved nothing – today even more of us are dying"

Suddenly one of them looked at my eldest son. My heart stopped. I didn't know whether it was the heat or the terror that covered my face in sweat. They asked my children's ages... "What do they study?...What do they care about? How do they spend their time?" I was burning. I just wanted them to leave.

I have three children; Sara, 22, Emad, 17 and Eyad, 15. One day, about a year ago, Eyad left to go to school. Half an hour later we heard a lot of shooting and the heavy rumble of explosions. Our normally quiet neighbourhood was thrown into turmoil. Our neighbour's daughter ran back home, screaming and shaking. There had been skirmishes and the Americans had invaded her high school to use it as a base from which to attack the armed militias. "Abu Emad, I want my son. I want him now" I shouted to my husband. I ran out into the street and waited there in my pyjamas until I finally saw him coming back with my son.

Everyday I say goodbye to my daughter and send her off to university. I kiss her and stand at the window praying she'll arrive safely. I call her several times while she's on her way. If I hear any explosions, I insist that she keep talking to me until she gets there.

I am torn. My life and that of my children is in Mosul – our house, our memories, everything that we know and that means anything to us. But, am I not being unfair to them if I choose to stay? And if I left, where would I go? What kind of future can I possibly offer them?

In the early hours of the morning, before the rest of the
house is awake, I steal a moment with my daughter and
all the struggles of the day ahead seem worthwhile.
My exhaustion melts away the moment I hear my children
calling 'Mum'. At home in Mosul

اصحو قبل ان يستيقظ من في البيت ، اسرق لحظات مع طفلتي فأشعر ان كل
ما سياتي من تعب يستحق . يتبدد تعبي في اللحظة التي اسمع فيها اطفالي
ينادونبي ماما بيتي في الموصل

I sit drinking my morning coffee and I get distracted.
I think about my daughter. She says to me "We're trapped
in the house and the terror in our streets is never-ending –
I'm just afraid that my future will end before all this does..."
I feel torn and deeply sad...I can try to find her work in
Erbil, but I'd collapse if she left my side. I would live in
constant terror of her being hurt. At home in Mosul

أجلس لأشرب قهوة الصباح.. وأشرد. أفكر بابنتي التي تكاد تختنق، تقول لي" الى متى
نظل حبيسي المنزل، والرعب في شوارعنا لا ينتهي.. أخشى أن ينتهي مستقبلي قبل أن
ينتهي كل هذا".. وأحزن أنا.. أتمزق.. يمكنني إرسالها لتعمل في أربيل، و لكني سأنهار
إن ابتعدت عني.. أخاف أن يصيبها سوء. بنتي في الموصل

Next page
Even if I'm tired and depressed, I jump out of bed at 7am.
I don't want my kids to be late for school or university.
I prepare breakfast, while they're getting dressed. I kiss
them goodbye and pretend to be very busy doing housework,
but deep inside I'm burning – praying that they reach their
schools safely. At home in Mosul

الصفحة السابقة
أقفز خارج سريري في السابعة صباحا، حتى وإن كنت متعبة أو محبطة، أخشى أن
يتأخر اطفالي على مدارسهم أو جامعاتهم. أحضر الفطور بينما يرتدون ملابسهم، أقبلهم
مودعة وأتظاهر أني مشغولة بأعمال المنزل، إلا أني في اعماقي أحترق وأصلي أن يصلوا
مدارسهم بسلام. بنتي في الموصل

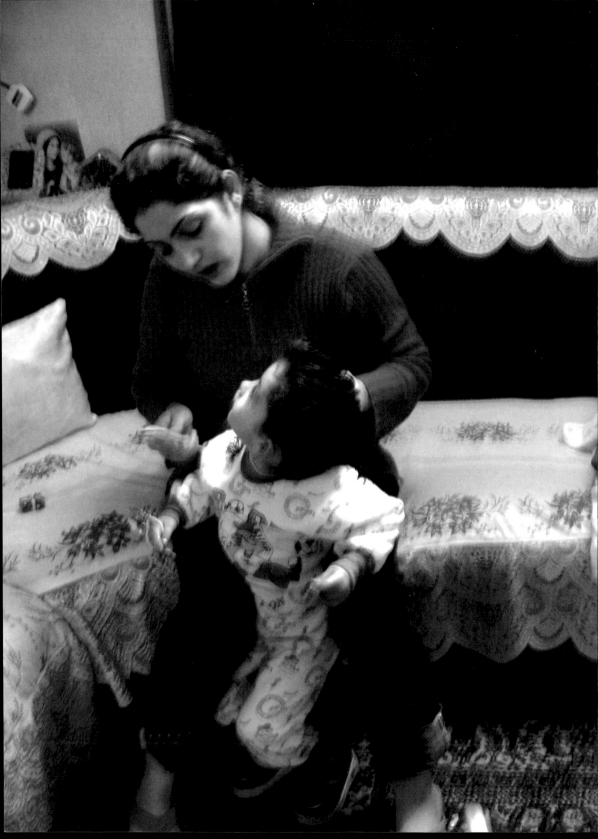

Previous page
My husband and I get home from work, tired. He sits and watches TV while I cook lunch and talk to the kids. Sara's graduating from university in a year's time and my two boys want to study outside Mosul. I try to keep them close. I'm afraid that the exhaustion of living in Iraq will make them drift away from each other and from me. At home in Mosul

الصفحة التالية

أصل أنا وزوجي من العمل متعبين..يجلس زوجي ليشاهد التلفاز وأنشغل أنا..
أحضر الغداء وأحادث الأطفال. سارة ستتخرج بعد عام ويريد ابناي الدراسة خارج
الموصل. أحاول دائما أن أخلق جسورا بينهم..أخشى أن الإرهاق وتعب العراق سيبعدهم
بعضهم عن بعض وعني. بيتي في الموصل

I was a very shy child. I used to be terrified of sounds and of the dark. I stammered until late into my teens. Since I became a mother all that has stopped. I will not allow anything – the explosions, or the armies, or anyone to implant fear in the hearts of my children. At home in Mosul

كنت طفلة شديدة الخجل.. أخاف من أي صوت ومن العتمة.. تأتأت حتى بلغت
الصبا. منذ أن أصبحت أما ، توقف كل هذا ، لن أسمح لأحد..لا للانفجارات ولا
للجيوش ولا لأي بشر أن يزرع الخوف في أولادي . بيتي في الموصل

I cook on the petrol stove; electricity
and gas have become dear visitors who
rarely honour us with their presence.
I help my kids with their studies, do
the laundry and keep an eye on the
food. It might take as much as four
hours to finish cooking. After coming
back from work the next day, I spend
an hour heating the meal. All this
work, but it means I can see my whole
family sitting down to a meal together,
just as we used to. At home in Mosul

أبدأ بتحضير طبختي بعد الظهر، أضعها على الموقد
النفطي، باتت الكهرباء و الغاز زوارا أعزاء نادرا ما
يشرفونا بحضورهم. أشاهد التلفاز.. أساعد أطفالي
في دراستهم.. أغسل الملابس.. وأنا أراقب الطبخة
التي قد تستغرق أربعة ساعات. بعد عودتي من
العمل في اليوم التالي أمضي ساعة في تسخينها
إلا أنها من الأشياء القلائل التي تجعل عائلتي اليوم
تجلس معا كما اعتدتها. بيتي في الموصل

I look out the window, watching the street and the faces of
the people in the cars. Strange thoughts go through my head
– maybe a car will stop and a terrorist will abduct my son for
ransom on his way home from the shop. Sometimes I wonder
how long we can go on living here, like this. So many families
have been forced to leave for one reason or another.
At home in Mosul

انظر من النافذة ,, اراقب الشارع.. أنظر في وجوه المارة، في السيارات البعيدة.. تنتابني
هواجس وأفكار غريبة.. ترعبني.. قد تقف تلك السيارة وينزل منها إرهابيون يختطفون
ابني وهو في طريقه من الدكان الى البيت للحصول على فدية.. اتساءل احيانا كم يمكننا
مواصلة العيش هكذا . اجبر الكثير على ترك بيوتهم لسبب او لآخر. بيتي في الموصل

Next page
Even in the few moments I steal for myself, I'm thinking
about my children. They stay up studying and working on
the computer. I lie in bed worrying about who will turn off
the generator; maybe a bullet will come from somewhere...
I can't fall asleep till I'm sure they've all gone to bed.
I don't want them to feel like I'm restricting them, but I
can't overcome my fear. At home in Mosul

الصفحة السابقة
أفكر في أولادي حتى في اللحظات التي أسرقها لأكون وحيدة. يبقون سهارى عندما
أذهب للنوم مساء.. يدرسون أو يعملون على الكمبيوتر.. وأفكر: من سيخرج ليطفئ
المولدة الكهربائية.. قد يوجد شخص ما هناك.. قد تنطلق رصاصة من مكان ما. لا
أغفو إلا بعد أن أدرك أنهم ذهبوا جميعا للنوم ، لا أريد أن أجعلهم يشعرون أني
أحاصرهم.. ولا أستطيع أن أتجاوز خوفي. بيتي في الموصل

الأمومة

سمعنا ضجيجا في الشارع، اقتربت وابنتي سارة من شباك المطبخ لنرى ما يحصل. رأيت ثلاث مدرعات أمريكية تجتاح شارعنا الضيق جدا.. تكسر الأشجار. وقف الجنود أمام منزلنا، ارتعبت، نظرت إلى سارة، ربما وقفوا لأن نظراتنا أزعجتهم.

أدركنا أنهم يفتشون المنطقة. كانت صواريخ قد أطلقت عليهم من منطقتنا في اليوم الفائت.

ركل الباب مرارا، خفت على أولادي، منعتهم من الاقتراب من الباب. ركض زوجي وفتح الباب.. دخلوا...جلسوا على أرائكنا. جلست وأولادي الثلاث على أريكة واحدة، كنت أرتعش.

"أمسيحيون أنتم؟" سأل أحدهم. أدركت أنهم قد لاحظوا الصليب المعلق على جداري.

"نعم"، أجاب زوجي.

"أتدعمون وجودنا هنا؟"

"لا.. لم تجلبوا لنا إلا الحرائق والدمار"

"أحببتم صدام؟"

"بالطبع لا.. حرق سنين عمرنا ثم جلبكم إلينا".

"والحكومة الحالية؟"

"لم تأت بجديد..اليوم نموت أكثر". كان زوجي يسخر بأسى.

فجأة.. نظر أحدهم إلى ولدي الأكبر، أحسست أن قلبي توقف، كان الطقس شديد الحرارة، ولا أعرف إن كان الحر أم الرعب هو الذي جعل العرق يغطي وجهي. سألوا عن أعمار أولادي.. بم يهتمون.. ماذا يدرسون.. كيف يقضون أيامهم. كنت أحترق، كل ما أردته هو أن يرحلوا.

عندي ثلاثة أولاد. سارة في الثانية والعشرين.. عماد في السابعة عشر من عمره، وعمر إياد خمسة عشر عاما. منذ ما يزيد على العام، خرج إياد إلى المدرسة. بعد نصف ساعة، بدأت أصوات إطلاق نار.. لم تتوقف.. تحولت في دقائق إلى انفجارات مرعبة. ارتبك شارعنا الهادئ عادة. رأيت ابنة جارتنا دنيا تعود راكضة تصرخ وترتجف، علمنا بعدها أن مواجهات قد نشبت بين الأمريكان وبعض المسلحين، واجتاح الأمريكان مدرستها الثانوية وتمركزوا فيها لضرب المسلحين. ذعرت...صرخت "أبو عماد ... أريد ابني...أريده الآن".

انتظرت في الشارع بملابس النوم... أرتجف وأصلي حتى رأيت ابني وزوجي.

. كل يوم أودع ابنتي في طريقها إلى الجامعة، أقبلها، أقف عند الشباك وأصلي أن تصل بسلام. أتصل بها أكثر من مرة لأكلمها، إذا سمعت صوت انفجار، أصر على أن تكلمني على الهاتف طوال الطريق.

أشعر أني أتمزق.

في الموصل حياتي وحياة أطفالي، بيتنا، ذكرياتنا ... كل ما نعرفه ويعني لنا، ولكن ... ألا أظلمهم بالبقاء...وإن غادرت، إلى أين أذهب؟... أي مستقبل يمكنني أن أمنحهم حينها ؟!

أنطوانيت – الموصل

كنت في صفي الاخير من الثانوية عندما اقترب موعد زواج أختي؛ بدأت الاحتفالات والولائم.

"أتعتقدين انك إن تخرجت من الجامعة ستعيلين الأسرة؟" كان هذا جواب أمي حين طلبت منها تخفيف أعبائي البيتية حتى أتمكن من الدراسة.

لم ادخل الجامعة وبدأت العمل.. كنت سعيدة.

عدت يوما إلى المنزل لأجد أسرة صديق أخي في منزلنا تطلب يدي، وفعلا تمت الخطبة.

عندما خطبت إلى نضال كان يؤدي الخدمة الإلزامية. ثم بدأت الحرب مع ايران ولم اعد أراه.. لم أكن اعرفه.. وددت أن انهي خطوبتي. هددني والدي عندما عرف برغبتي قائلا "أذبحك.. بناتنا لا يفعلن هذا".

بعد مرور عامين ونصف، أدركنا أن الحرب لن تنتهي قريبا.. قررنا الزواج بأي حال. أمضى معي أسبوعا واحدا بعد الزفاف، ثم عاد الى الثكنة العسكرية. كان يعيش في الموصل وكنت مع اسرتي في بغداد.. تابعت عملي ولم أره في نصف العام الاول من زواجنا سوى ثلاث مرات. وبعد ذلك استقلت من عملي ولحقت بزوجي في الموصل.

كان الوضع نسبيا أفضل.. أصبحت أراه مرة كل أسبوع.. بعد عامين ولدت سارة..

عرفت من التلفاز ان الحرب قد انتهت.. قفزت فرحا ونسيت أني حامل. عاد زوجي إلى المنزل، كانت المرة الأولى التي يبقى فيها برفقتي.. لكن وفي عام 1991، أخذ مني ثانية، عند بدء حرب الخليج الثانية. قالوا إن صدام قد ينفذ تهديده ويستهدف إسرائيل، حينها سيفقد الأمريكان صوابهم ويضربوننا بالاسلحة الكيميائية. وبدأنا نستعد لكل الاحتمالات؛ بعضنا وضع الشريط اللاصق العريض على شكل حرف X فوق كل نافذة، لئلا تتشظى النوافذ، وتؤذي أحدا في حال كسرت.. البعض الآخر عمل على تخزين الماء، حضرنا علب الإسعاف وقطع الشاش المحشوة بالقطن والفحم لاستخدامها كمامات حماية، في حال حصول أي هجوم كيميائي على الرغم من أن مخاوفنا وكوابيسنا من الكيميائي لم تتحقق، إلا أنهم حولوا السما.. إلى دخان اسود كثيف.. حرائق وانفجارات ومطر اسود. ولدت ابني، كان أسمر بعكس إخوته، وضحكنا معلقين: "ربما الدخان سوّد بشرته".

بدأ الحصار، وكانت أياما صعبة.. كنا نراقب الأفواه. بعنا كل ما نملك؛ المصوغات، الأثاث.. ثم ملابسنا. في سنوات الحصار التحقت بالجامعة. شعرت أن حلمي القديم بدأ يتحقق. كنت أسير إلى الجامعة محتضنة كتبي, وابنتي تسير بجانبي في طريقها الى مدرستها الثانوية.

في 2003-4-9، كنا نجلس في بيت عائلة زوجي نشاهد تمثال صدام يسقط.. كانت دموعي تنهمر بصمت.. راقبت أطفالي الثلاثة. كانت وجوههم حزينة.

"أتبكين على صدام؟" غضبت أخت زوجي !

"بالعكس، ابكي دمارا أراه محتم القدوم الى وطني"

الأمومة

SLEEPLESS

MARIAM, FALLUJA

My brother, Marwan, was sixteen when he was arrested, accused of killing a man, who we'd taken pity on and given work to...after searching all the police stations, we finally found him, his shirt stained with blood and there were burns all over his body...after so much torture, my brother confessed to a crime he didn't commit and was sentenced to ten years in prison...my older brother Ziad was accused of being an accomplice and sentenced to death even though he was in Kuwait doing his military service. He was withdrawn from the front and imprisoned for six months. We knew he was being tortured...my mother cried the whole time...

Marwan was released in my second year of university and we believed that joy would finally come back into our lives... One day, my friend and I were chatting in our garden...we heard a car screech to a halt...my blood ran cold...I remembered how my father had been hit by a car and killed...then I heard the gunshots...the family of the boy my brother had been accused of killing, killed my older brother, Ziad, in revenge...my mother ran out into the street, barefoot...without covering her head...we ran after her...the police closed off the area...they didn't let us get close to him...Ziad was taken away in an ambulance...my mother stood looking at a pool of his blood, not knowing what to say...she sat down on the ground...and without being aware of it she steeped her hands in my brother's blood and beat her head... and her face...and her breast – screaming "oh my son, my son."

In my last year of university...they tried to make us learn how to use guns... I always ran away from the training...I'm afraid of guns.

"Baghdad has fallen"...we heard it on the radio...a year later in April 2004 the Americans invaded Falluja...I remember my brother saying that the tribal leaders would never accept the shame, or allow them to search our houses or our women. At first we thought there would only be fighting on the streets...then the electricity was cut...the phone rang: "Your cousin, Ahmed, has been killed"...I locked the door so no one could leave the house, but my brother wrenched the key from my hand and they all ran towards my cousin's house...I tried to stop my uncle from going... he pushed me to one side and ran out...just a few minutes later the phone rang again "Someone has been killed right outside your door". My mother and I ran out the door...she screamed: "They've killed Abdulwahab"...the sniper lowered his gun... I approached my uncle's body...he looked like he was sleeping...after my own father died, my uncle Abdulwahab had become like a father to me...he taught me about all the countries he'd visited.

Finally, I presented my master's thesis. I was beaming until I glanced over to the empty chair where my uncle should have been.

SLEEPLESS

April 2004...The Americans bombed Falluja...For three days, we crowded into the innermost room in the house, windowless and furthest from the street and a sniper's bullet...I heard our neighbours next door packing frantically...We fled, a white flag flying from the car window...all escape routes out of the city were blocked by the occupation...We slept outdoors, sharing our bread with another family - and they gave us water...Finally, the Euphrates River offered a way out...It was calm enough for the men to swim across - the women, children and old people crossed by canoe... We went to my grandfather's house in Koubeis.

I counted the minutes and hours till I could go home...Finally they said we could. We were under siege – barbed wire, concrete walls and innumerable American checkpoints everywhere...I felt like my city had been transformed into a huge concentration camp...My brother told me that when the bombing had stopped, they'd combed the city arresting or killing whoever was still alive...the municipality buried the bodies that filled the streets, and moved the corpses buried in people's gardens to the cemetery...And I thought to myself: "The dead should be honoured with a proper burial, but during the invasion we were forced to bury our dead in our gardens"...The stench of death filled the streets...They changed Falluja into a city of ghosts...We arrived home...Everything was smashed – couches, beds, electrical machines...Our neighbour, Um Abdullah, found her husband's decaying body on their bed when she got back...We started re-building our houses but we were besieged and isolated from the rest of the world...

Less than seven months later, we heard a voice shouting over a loudspeaker "If we find any man here under the age of 45, he will be killed"...We left our house... what happened this time was even uglier...The Americans and the National Guard set our houses on fire – like candles to light their way...My graduation pictures were burned, everything was burned. They killed everybody, even an old man who was praying in the mosque...Not even the house of God was safe from them...

People sifted through the ruins of their houses, face and hands covered in ash... We collected the charred remains of our possessions and started yet again to re-build our houses...We tried to feel alive again...We were invited to my cousin's wedding in Syria...My brother and a cousin stayed behind to guard the house...Two days later, my cousin, Mohammed, was killed by the Americans as he went out the door...He was shot in the leg and, as he tried to crawl away, they opened fire riddling his body with bullets – like a sieve...They raided the house later, shooting their guns off in every which way...His wife clutched their baby and screamed and screamed...

The Americans occupied our house at 3 am...I woke to my cousin's screams... a laser beam from a soldier's gun shone in the middle of her forehead...I grabbed a sheet to cover my head...I've now moved my bed to face the door...I don't sleep...

Another night of heavy shooting and gunfire in Falluja...
I try to sleep but I can't...my nights are invaded by the
quiet agonies kept at bay during the day...I get out of bed...
I pace up and down my room...who will we be crying over
in the morning? At home in Falluja

ليلة اخرى من الضرب واصوات إ طلاق رصاص عالي .. أحاول النوم ولا أستطيع.. . الآم
النهار تغزو ليالي . اخرج من فراشي واروح واغدي بالغرفة .. من سننعى في الصباح

بيتي بالفلوجة

Next page

Everybody is sleeping. I wander around the house, quietly
make tea and sit at the kitchen table. These are the bullet
holes in the wall of our kitchen...it opens onto the terrace...
during the first invasion of Falluja we were unable to enter
the kitchen for days...the snipers shot anything they could
see moving.... At home in Falluja

الصفحة السابقة

كل من في البيت نائم .. ادور في البيت .. بهدوء اعد شايا واضعه على طاولة المطبخ
هذا جدار مطبخي.. يطل المطبخ على باحة المنزل الخارجية.. أثناء الاجتياح الأول للفلوجة،
لم نتمكن من الوصول إلى المطبخ لأيام... كان القناص يستهدف كل ما يتحرك...

بيتي بالفلوجة

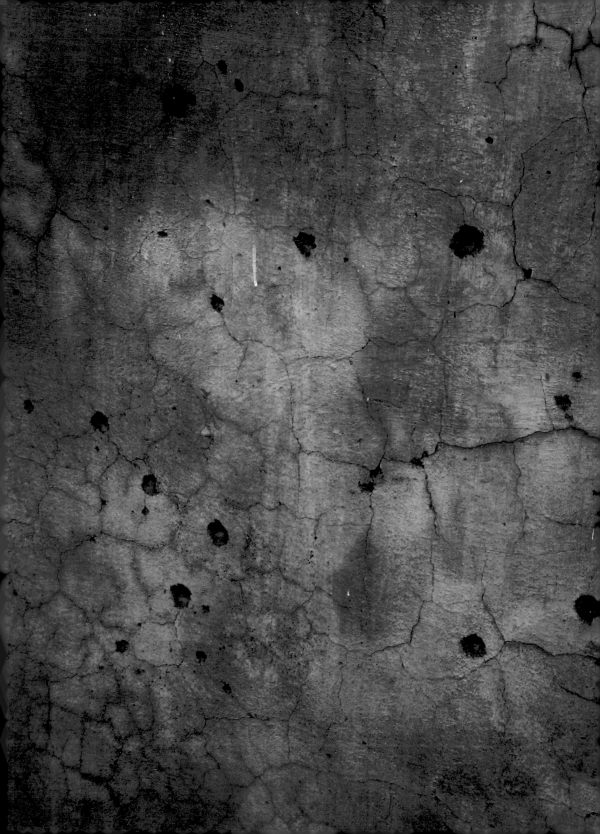

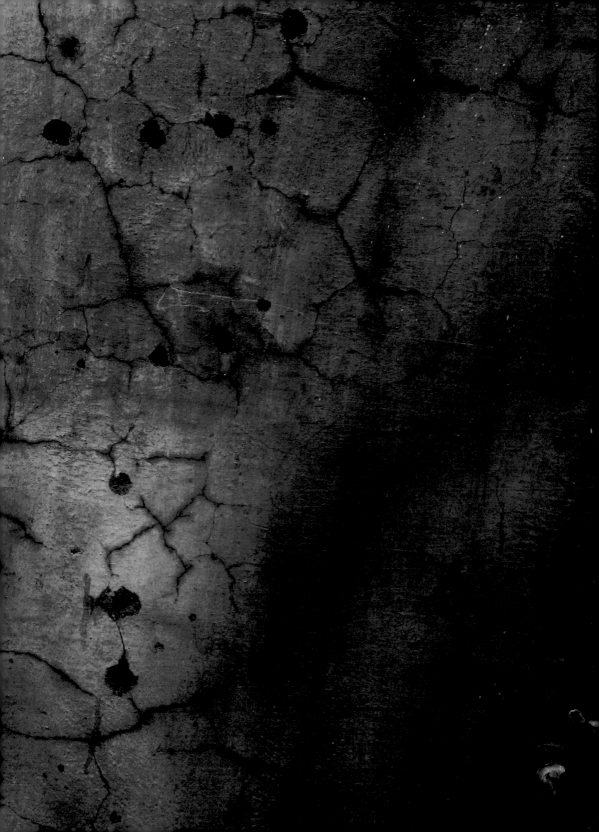

The Americans occupied our house more than once...in
the black of night...they came...they kicked in the doors...
suddenly they were standing above us...all night I wander
around the house shoving tables in front of all the doors...
so I'll hear them when they come. At home in Falluja

داهم الأمريكان منزلنا أكثر من مرة.. في عتمة الليل أتوا.. ركلوا الأبواب... ، فوجئت بهم
فوق رؤوسنا.. اليوم لا أذهب إلى النوم ، إلا بعد ان أتأكد أني وضعت طاولة خلف كل
باب.. على أن أتنبه عند دخولهم.. بيتي بالفلوجة

Next page
I surrender to my bed...I lie down and feel the discomfort of
the crumpled sheets...the room is stuffy and I want to open
a window, but I can't. I close my eyes and try to sleep...the
sound of guns fills my static room and I open my eyes again
– for hours and hours I stare at the ceiling of my room...
At home in Falluja

الصفحة السابقة
استلقي في فراشي . اشعر بتجعيدة شرشف السرير .الغرفة تخنقني .. أريد فتح النافذة
لكني لا استطيع اغلق عيني .. أحاول النوم.. أصوات النار تملأ جمود عالمي، ويغزوني
القلق.. لساعات وساعات أحدق في سقف الغرفة بيتي بالفلوجة

When they raid our house, I become paralyzed – like a piece of wood. I don't know how to react. They leave in the darkness, just as they came in the darkness...I have moved my bed to face the door...will they come back tonight?
At home in Falluja

عندما يقتحمون بيتنا أتخشب .. لا أتمكن من الحراك. . يغادرون في الظلام مثلما
يأتون في الظلام .. وضعت سريري مقابل الباب.. أنام وعيني تراقب الباب.. ..
هل سيأتون الليلة أيضا ؟ بيتي في الفلوجة

Next page
The gunfire pulls me out of bed...I want to know what's happening...I go to the kitchen window...I forget for a few moments that I might be shot...by them...picked out by their flares...for a second or two I don't remember the bullet holes in the door... At home in Falluja

الصفحة السابقة
تنتزعني أصوات إطلاق نار. من فراشي.. أحاول معرفة ما يحدث.. أركض نحو نافذة المطبخ
.. أنسى للحظات أنني يمكن أن أكون هدفا .. لهم.. لنيرانهم.. أغفل للحظات عن ثقب
الرصاصة في الباب.. بيتي بالفلوجة

Previous page
I drape my black shawl in front of the camera...I feel I only
see in darkness now. At home in Falluja

الصفحة التالية
وضعت شالي الأسود على عدسة الكاميرا .. صرت لا أرى الأشياء إلا معتمة. بيتي بالفلوجة

I can't work, I can't go anywhere - God didn't create us so
we would be buried alive inside our houses – we want to
be free, we want to live our lives. The world is bigger than
this tiny space I wander in somewhere between sleep and
consciousness...between night and day. At home in Falluja

لا استطيع العمل .. لا استطيع الذهاب الى اي مكان . لم يخلقنا الله كي يدفننا
احياء في بيوتنا . نريد ان نكون احرارا .. نريد ان نحيا حياتنا . الحياة اكبر من هذا
المكان الصغير الذي اسير فيه بين النوم واليقظة .. بين الليل والنهار . بيتي بالفلوجة

الأرق

في نيسان 2004، اجتاح الأمريكان مدينتي.. كان القصف شديدا.. لأيام ثلاث، لم نكن قادرين على مغادرة الصالة الداخلية البعيدة عن الشارع والنوافذ، لئلا يصطادنا قناص.. سمعت أصوات جيراننا وهم يجمعون أشياءهم مغادرين.. تركنا بيتنا بعدها نحن أيضا، واضعين الراية البيضاء على سيارتنا.. أمضينا أياما نحاول إيجاد منفذ للخروج من المدينة، التي أغلقها الاحتلال.. نمنا في العراء.. تقاسمنا أرغفة الخبز مع أسر شاركتنا العراء وما تبقى لديها من ماء.. نهر الفرات كان أخيرا عوننا على المغادرة.. كان هادئا بينما كان الأولاد القادرون على السباحة يقطعونه، وقطعته وأمي والأطفال في قارب.. ذهبنا إلى كبيسة.. إلى منزل جدي..

"يمكنكم العودة الآن".. لم أكن مصدقة.. كنت أعد الدقائق والساعات للعودة.. وصلنا أطراف المدينة.

وجدت المدينة محاصرة بحزام من الأسلاك الشائكة والحواجز الكونكريتية، وبعدد، بدا لانهائيا، من نقاط التفتيش الأمريكية.... شعرت أنهم حولوا مدينتي إلى معتقل كبير.. أخبرني أخي أنهم، وبعد نهاية المعارك، مشطوا المدينة.. اعتقلوا أو قتلوا كل من بقي حيا.. أدخلوا البلدية لتدفن بقايا الجثث، التي ملأت الشوارع، ونقل في دفن المعارك أثناء البيوت، إلى المقبرة.. وفكرت: إكرام الميت دفنه، حتى هذا الإكرام لم يتحقق لنا، لأننا أجبرنا على دفن شهدائنا في حدائق بيوتنا .. كانت رائحة الموت تملأ المدينة.. لقد حولوا الفلوجة إلى مدينة أشباح.

وصلت إلى المنزل، كان كل ما امتلكناه مدمرا، الأرائك والأسرة والأجهزة الكهربائية.. أخبرتنا جارتنا أم عبد الله أنها وجدت زوجها جثة متفسخة على فراشها عندما عادت إلى منزلها.

بدأنا بإعمار بيوتنا، إلا أننا شعرنا أننا محاصرين ومعزولين عن بقية العالم .

بعد أقل من سبعة أشهر، سمعنا صوتا يصرخ في مكبر الصوت: "إن وجدنا أي رجل دون 54، سيقتل". غادرنا منزلنا. ما حدث هذه المرة كان أبشع، كان الأمريكان والحرس الوطني يشعلون بيوتنا، مثل الشموع، لتنير يوم دربهم.. احترقت صوري.. صور تخرجي.. كل شيء احترق، حتى عجوزا كان يصلي في المسجد.. لم تسلم بيوت الله من أذاهم.

أذكر عند العودة، رؤية العوائل وهي تتفقد بقايا بيوتها .. أذكر الرماد الذي غطى وجوههم وأيديهم. لملمنا الأكوام المحروقة، وعدنا مرة أخرى لنعمر بيوتنا.. حاولنا أن نحس الحياة من جديد.

دعينا وعائلة عمي لحضور زفاف ابن عمي الآخر في سوريا. بقي أخي وابن عمي في البيوت لحمايتها. بعد يومين، قتل الأمريكان محمد ابن عمي عندما كان يغادر المنزل. أصابوه في قدمه أولا، وعندما زحف محاولا النجاة، أمطروه بوابل من الرصاص .. بدا جسده كالمنخل.. هاجموا منزله. فتحوا نيرانهم في كل اتجاه.. كانت زوجته تصرخ وهي تحتضن طفلها.

داهموا منزلنا الساعة الثالثة ليلا.. استيقظت على صوت ابنة عمي تصرخ وليزر الجندي الأمريكي على وجهها.. رفعت الشراشف.. أردت أن أغطي شعري.. منذ ذلك اليوم.. غيرت مكان سريري ليكون بمواجهة الباب.. ولا أنام ..

مريم- الفلوجة

كان أخي مروان في السادسة عشر من عمره يوم اعتقلوه.. ، اتهم أخي بقتل عامل كنا قد عطفنا عليه ومنحناه عملا لدينا لأسبوع.. بعد أن بحثنا عنه في كل مركز للشرطة.. جيء بقميصه ملطخا بالدماء وعليه أثار حروق.. تمكنا أخيرا من زيارته.. بعد كثير من التعذيب، وقع أخي اعترافا خطيا على جرم لم يقترفه.. حكم عليه بعشر سنوات سجن.. الغريب أن أخي الأخر زياد ، الذي كان يؤدي الخدمة العسكرية في الكويت حينها، حوكم غيابيا بالإعدام!! ساقوه من الجبهة إلى السجن، ولزمنا ستة اشهر لنثبت براءته، ويطلق سراحه.. كنا نعرف ما كانا يتعرضان إليه.. كنت أرى أمي تبكي طوال الوقت.

أطلق سراح أخي مروان وانا في عامي الثاني من الجامعة .

كنت وصديقتي نتسامر في باحة الدار..سمعت صوت إطارات سيارة مسرعة تتوقف فجأة.. خفت.. كان والدي قد قتل في حادث سيارة.. سمعت إطلاق صوت نار.. أسرة الصبي، الذي اتهم أخي بقتله، قتلت أخي زياد.. ركضت أمي حافية.. بلا حجاب.. ونحن نركض خلفها.. كانت الشرطة تطوق المكان.. لم يسمحوا لنا بالاقتراب منه.. نقل زياد بسيارة إسعاف.. بقيت أمي بمواجهة بركة دم زياد لا تعرف ما تفعل.. جلست على الأرض.. من دون وعي كانت تغطس كفيها بدم أخي.. تلطخ فيه رأسها، وجهها.. ، وصدرها وهي تصرخ "ولدي.. ولدي".

في السنة الأخيرة من الجامعة.. كان يفترض بي التدرب على السلاح.. كنت دائما أهرب من التدريب.. أخاف من السلاح.. احتلت بغداد عندما كنت اعمل على كتابة رسالة الماجستير.. سمعنا الخبر في الراديو "سقطت بغداد".. كنا قلقين.. لا نعرف ما سيحدث.. بعدها بفترة، في نيسان 2004 ، اجتاح الأمريكان مدينتنا.. أتذكر أخي يخبرني " لن يقبل شيوخ العشائر بهذا العار، لن يسمحوا لهم بتفتيش بيوتنا ونسائنا".

اعتقدنا أنها مناوشات كالتي تحدث يوميا.. بعد ساعات قطعت الكهربا.. صباح اليوم التالي رن الهاتف "قتل ابن عمك احمد".. أقفلت الباب خائفة على الجميع، إلا أن أخي انتزع المفتاح من يدي.. ركض وابن عمي باتجاه بيت القتيل.. حاولت منع خالي من اللحاق بهم.. دفعني وغادر مسرعا.. بعدها بدقائق رن الهاتف مرة أخرى "احدهم مقتول على باب منزلكم".. ركضنا أمي وأنا.. صرخت أمي " قتل عبد الوهاب " اقتربت من خالي.. أنزل القناص سلاحه.. بدا خالي نائما.. عندما مات والدي صار خالي عبد الوهاب يملأ أيامي..

قدمت رسالة الماجستير..كنت أبتسم إلا أنني كنت أراقب كرسي خالي الفارغ..

الأرق

BITTER

UM MOHAMMED, BASRA

We moved to a smaller house, but it felt big because we were happy there. When the war with Iran began, my brother put on his army uniform and left for the front. The joy drained out of the house.

There was a knock at the door; my brother had been killed. My mother screamed, tore her clothes and ran out into the street – barefoot. We ran after her. She was not conscious of herself - lost. Later we discovered he'd been wounded in the leg and was lying in hospital in Nasiriya. The injury saved his life and he was never sent to the front again.

We'd hardly caught our breath, before we found ourselves in the middle of yet another war. The Iraqi army had occupied Kuwait. Seven months later, they were defeated. I remember our soldiers returning; their feet were swollen, they'd walked the muddy roads all the way home, and the fighter planes had continued to bomb them even after the ceasefire had been declared.

Encouraged by America, uprisings against the government began in the immediate aftermath of the war. My youngest brother, Fadhil, joined and I followed, not because I was opposed to the regime, but because I was frightened for him. I was shot.

Helicopter gun-ships flew over our heads, above them hovered the American planes – watching. Day after day, artillery fire rained down on us. The regime stayed in power and arrested thousands of people. My brother was sentenced to death. They tortured him badly, he confessed to nothing. We paid bribes and used any influence we had to get him out. I hugged him and he winced with pain. He'd been beaten with cables. They'd hung him from his feet.

I married and was about to deliver my second child when my brother was arrested again. They said they would hang everyone who'd participated in the uprising. My family rushed to comfort my mother. Alone in the house, that night, I gave birth to my baby girl. The umbilical was wrapped around her neck. She cried twice and then she died. The sanctions had ground us down and Iraq had become a very small place to live in.

We decided to emigrate. We gave all our money to a friend so she could change it into dollars for us. We never saw that 'friend' again. So, we rented a house in Baghdad and lived there.

Three years later, the Americans decided to "liberate Iraq". Sahaf, the Minister of Information, appeared on TV: "We will repel those animals". Those "animals" managed to occupy Baghdad in just three weeks. Minutes after George W. Bush declared "Operation Iraqi Freedom", thirty-nine rockets shattered the silence of the city's night.

BITTER

As the first bombs fell in the middle of the night, I threw my children's things into the car. We fled Baghdad to return to my city – to Basra – to safety.

Some people in the new local government had had strong connections with Iran during the time of Saddam. They promised that things would be different. They said times had changed. They didn't speak in our accent and their private conversations were often in Farsi. Everyday there were more and more foreigners. And everyday the piles of rubbish grew.

I started the Basra Women's Union. When I'd come home from work, my three children would greet me at the door, their faces blank with boredom in our desolate house - empty of everything but beds and mats on the floor.

I walked through Um Al Broom Square – I couldn't believe it - the Karnak Cinema was a bombed out, ruined skeleton. I saw so many films there when I was young.

The amusement park near our house was looted and all the rides destroyed by people stealing the metal and brick. Even the palm trees were set alight. The last time I passed by there, I saw that instead of children playing there were grazing sheep. And in place of the green lawn, there were heaps of garbage drowning in stagnant water.

Basra was always full of life and open to new ideas. I remember poetry readings and concerts at the Cultural Center, listening to popular music and watching dance performances. Now, since the occupation, the religious parties have taken over all the buildings in Basra. Everything is black now; the mourning banners for martyrs – for those who are dying now and for Imam Hussein, who died more than 1300 years ago.

Women are compelled to wear black robes and veil their faces.

There are only men on the streets, with their pock-marked faces, looking at me with rage. Their beards look dirty, lice-ridden.

One morning I found a leaflet shoved under my door. "Sinner, stop your work. You and your daughter must wear proper hijab…" I noticed the spelling was bad. Everything in Basra is forbidden now: laughter, coloured clothes, music, walking in the markets, going to the parks. Everything beautiful has been stolen from my city.

And the British who came in the name of liberating Iraq, just watch it all, smiling. Yes, we have been freed from life and we have begun a mourning, whose end we do not know.

Previous page
This is old Basra...now...I remember
how I loved its houses and its shanashil
(balconies)...its river with the boats
plying up and down...nothing is left
of it but ruin and destruction, broken
bricks, collapsing houses. Everyday,
the river shrinks - it's full of garbage.
The old city, Basra

الصفحة التالية
هذه هي البصرة القديمة.. الآن أذكر كم كنت أحبها.. أحب
بيوتها وشناشيلها.. نهرها بقواربه الذاهبة والغادية. لم
يتبق من البصرة القديمة الآن إلا خرائب.. طابوق محطم
وبيوت تكاد تنهار.. واختفت سعة النهر.. ملأته القمامة.
المدينة القديمة – البصرة

This place used to be full of life.
I used to love walking down the
Corniche holding the hands of my
children and talking to my friends.
Today, the Corniche is empty. Men and
women walking together are asked to
prove that they are relatives or husband
and wife. Now the place is full of the
hum of traffic. The Corniche Shat Al Arab,
Basra

كان هذا المكان يعج بالحياة. لطالما أحببت المشي هنا
مسكة بيد طفلي وأنا أتحدث إلى إحدى الصديقات.
اليوم..الكورنيش فارغ، يطلب من أي رجل وامرأة يسيران
معا إظهار ما يثبت أنهما قريبان أو زوجان.. الان لاشيء
سوى ضجيج السيارات كورنيش شط العرب – البصرة

Previous page

The last time I visited this building,
my husband and I met up with a group
of writers and artists. This used to
be a busy cultural centre. Today, as
everywhere else in Basra, it has been
taken over by one of the religious
parties, which have swallowed up
my city since the beginning of the
occupation. They put their black
flag in the mouth of the dragon,
announcing the death of happiness.
A former cultural centre, Basra

الصفحة التالية

آخر مرة زرت فيها هذا المبنى.. التقيت وزوجي بمجموعة
من الكتاب والفنانين. كان هذا المبنى مركزا ثقافيا..
اليوم..مثل البصرة بأسرها، بات هذا المبنى مقرا لأحد
الأحزاب الدينية. ابتلعت هذه الأحزاب مدينتي بأسرها بعد
الاحتلال.. ووضعوا علمهم الأسود في فم التنين معلنين
قدوم موت جديد. بناية لمركز ثقافي سابق – البصرة

I was five years old when my uncle
took me to see 'Abla and Antar'at the
Al Karnak Cinema. When I grew up,
I'd stop to look at posters of the stars
and advertisements for coming films.
After the occupation began, those
who wanted to end the 'corrupting'
influence of films, demolished
the cinema. The Al Karnak Cinema, Basra

كنت في الخامسة من عمري عندما أخذني خالي إلى هذه
السينما.. كانت الكثير من العوائل قد اصطحبت أطفالها إلى
سينما الكرنك لمشاهدة فيلم "عنتر وعبلة". عندما كبرت كنت
أتوقف، كلما ذهبت الى العمل، عند صور نجمات السينما
ونجومها.. إعلانات الأفلام المعروضة.. بعد الاحتلال انهى
"الآمرون بالمعروف والناهون عن المنكر" فساد الأفلام ودمروا
السينما !!! سينما الكرنك – البصرة

The religious men who are running my city, on behalf of God, have destroyed the statues of the city because they say they are haram (forbidden). Women's bodies are 'shameful', it seems, even if they are made of brass. Tayaran Square in Basra.

ساحة الطيران في البصرة ، حاول القائمون بأمر الله على مدينتي، تدمير التماثيل بحجة انها حرام.. استهدفوا تمثال المرأة وتركوا تماثيل الرجل والسمكة بسلام.. جسد المرأة عورة حتى وان كان من نحاس!! ساحة الطيران – البصرة

Next page
Everything in my city has been looted, stolen and burned and the British army has just laughed and called the thieves the Ali Babas of Basra. We visited this ruined piece of land many times when it was an amusement park. After the occupation, the rides were all stolen, even the bricks. And, for some inexplicable reason, the palm trees were burned. A former amusement park, Basra

الصفحة السابقة
سرق كل ما في مدينتي و دمر أو حرق .. جلس الجنود البريطانيون مراقبين وهم يضحكون.. سموا اللصوص "علي بابا البصرة".. زرت هذه الأرض الخربة مرات يوم كانت مدينة للألعاب. بعد الاحتلال..سرقت كل الألعاب.. حتى الطابوق..ولسبب غامض حرق نخلها!! مدينة الالعاب في البصرة سابقا

Basra's people were martyred in
the Iran-Iraq war...in the Gulf War...
in the uprising against Saddam
Hussein...in the bombing during
the occupation of the country...and
they are still being martyred, now by
terrorist militias, by the British...this
young man is sitting talking to a loved
one who has been killed. Al Hassan Al
Basri Cemetery, Basra

استشهد أهل البصرة.. في الحرب الايرانية العراقية،
واستشهدوا في حرب الخليج.. واستشهدوا في
الانتفاضة..واستشهدوا في الحصار..ثم استشهدوا في
قصف الاحتلال.. ولا يزالون يستشهدون اليوم على يد
الإرهابيين.. والميليشيات، والبريطانيين. يجلس هذا الشاب
مخاطبا عزيزا قد قتل. مقبرة الحسن البصري – البصرة

Next page
I came back to Basra from Baghdad
the day the invasion began. I loved my
city and was proud to be from there.
It used to be a crossroads of people and
cultures, a place of warmth, beauty and
elegance, generous-hearted and open
to the whole world. Now, everything
we loved about the city has been taken
from us; it is not the place it was and
I feel the bitterness of this loss.
By the Al Ashar river, Basra

الصفحة السابقة
عدت من بغداد إلى البصرة في اليوم الأول للاحتلال..
أحببت مدينتي، ولطالما افتخرت بانتمائي إليها..
كانت البصرة دائما مركز جذب للكثير من الأشخاص
والحضارات... مكانا حميما وأنيقا.. اليوم..سلب منا كل
ما أحببناه في المدينة ..لم تعد البصرة التي عرفت.. مرارة
هذه الخسارة تعصر قلبي.عند نهر العشار – البصرة

المرارة

في منتصف الليل، لملمت أغراض أطفالي على عجل.. غادرت بغداد وصواريخ الحرب، التي أعلنت منذ أيام، تضربها . أردت الذهاب إلى مدينتي.. إلى البصرة.. فهناك أماني .

بدأت العمل في منظمة تعني بالمرأة، اعتدت، وكل زملائي، حضور اجتماع أسبوعي مع أحد مسئولي المحافظة، كانوا يعدوننا بالتغيير.. كانوا يقولون إن الزمن اختلف . كان معظم هؤلاء يتكلم بلكنة غريبة . وحواراتهم الخاصة تدور بالفارسية . كان الغرباء يزدادون يوما بعد آخر.. وأكوام القمامة ترتفع شيئا فشيئا ..

كل مرة عدت فيها من العمل، استقبلني أطفالي الثلاثة بوجوه يأكلها الملل، في منزل فارغ إلا من بعض الحصر والفرش ... أتساءل : أين عساني أن آخذهم !! بعد أشهر من عودتي ، كنت أمشي في ساحة أم البروم، عندما فوجئت أن سينما الكرنك؛ السينما التي زرتها مرارا في صباي، قد أصبحت أنقاضا . مدينة الألعاب، المكان المحبب لدى الأطفال عادة، نهبت، دمرت كل ألعابها، لأن احدهم أراد الاستفادة من حديدها أو طابوقها، حتى نخلها حرق . المرة الأخيرة، التي مررت قريبا، كانت قد استبدلت أطفالها بأغنام ترعى، وبدل مرجها الأخضر، وجدت تلالا من القمامة تغوص في مياه آسنة .

كانت البصرة دائما حية.. ثقافتها متجددة. أذكر كل تلك الأماسي التي كنا نقضيها في المركز الثقافي، نحضر قراءات شعرية أو حفلة موسيقية ، نستمع لأغانينا الشعبية.. الخشابة ونشاهد رقصة الهيوا ..

بعد الاحتلال، ما عاد في البصرة من مكان إلا ما كان للأحزاب الدينية.. المركز الثقافي بات حصة أحدها .. أمسى كل شيء، أسودا . اليافطات التي تنعي الشهداء سوداء .. شهداء اليوم.. والحسين الذي أستشهد منذ ما يفوق 1300 عام.. فرض على النساء ارتداء عباءات ويراقع سود . صارت حياتي سوداء .. صارت شيئا فشيئا لم أعد أرى في الشوارع سوى رجال بوجوه كالحة يرمقونني بغضب . أشعر أن لحاهم تملؤها القاذورات وبعشش فيها القمل.

استيقظت ذات صباح لأجد ورقة دست من تحت الباب "توقفي عن عملك وارتدي أنت وابنتك الحجاب يا فاسقة" كتب على الورقة، كل ما استرعى انتباهي حينها هو الأخطاء الإملائية الكثيرة.

بات كل شيء في البصرة حرام، الضحكة، والملابس الملونة، والموسيقا، والتجول في الأسواق، وزيارة المتنزهات.. سرق كل شيء جميل في مدينتي. الحياة والمباني، والبريطانيون الذين أتوا باسم "الحرية للعراق"، يراقبون مبتسمين.

نعم، لقد حررنا من الحياة.. وبدأنا حدادا لا نعرف متى ينتهي.

أم محمد – البصرة

انتقلنا من بيت العائلة الكبير إلى بيت صغير خاص بنا كبر بسعادتنا، إلا أن الحرب العراقية الإيرانية أطبقت على خناقنا، وغادر الفرح بيتنا وأنا أرى أخي يغادره مرتديا بزته العسكرية إلى نار جبهات القتال.

كنا نجلس في المنزل.. دق الباب.. كان صديقاً لأخي، أتى يخبرنا بان أخي قد قتل. صرخت أمي ومزقت ثيابها وركضت إلى الشارع حافية، ونحن نركض وراءها.. كانت تركض بلا وعي .عرفنا بعدها أنه مصاب بإحدى ساقيه ويرقد في مستشفى في الناصرية، إصابته أنقذت حياته، ولم يرسل إلى الجبهة مرة أخرى.

لم نكد نلتقط أنفاسنا، حتى دخلنا حربا أخرى.. احتل الجيش العراقي الكويت.. بعد أشهر سبع، هزم الجيش.. مازلت أتذكر جنودا عائدين منهكين بأقدام تورمت من المشي في طرق موحلة، بينما كانت الطائرات الأمريكية مستمرة بقصفهم حتى بعد سريان إيقاف إطلاق النار.. كانت الانتفاضة قد انطلقت حينها، خرج أخي الأصغر فاضل مشاركا فيها. لحقت به، ليس لمعارضتي للنظام، بل خوفا على أخي.. أصيبت بطلق ناري..

بدأت المدفعية تضرب يوما بعد آخر، وكانت الطائرات السمتية تحلق فوق رؤوسنا، ترسل الموت إلى مدننا، و كانت الطائرات الأمريكية تحلق فوق السمتيات مباشرة وكأنها تحميها منا!! استعاد النظام قبضته من جديد، واعتقل العديد. صدر حكم الإعدام بحق أخي، لم يعترف أخي بشيء، رغم ما تعرض له من تعذيب. دفعنا الرشى، ولجأنا إلى وساطات عدة.. كنت سعيدة برؤيته يدخل البيت.. احتضنته بقوة.. تأوه متألما.. كان جسده متقرحا من الضرب بالكيبل.. كانوا يعلقونه من ساقيه..

تزوجت وأنجبت، كانت سنة سعيدة. عدت بعدها إلى العمل، لم يتوقف رجال الأمن عن ملاحقتي. تعبت.. استقلت من الوظيفة وقررت إكمال دراستي الجامعية.

اقترب موعد ولادة طفلتي الثانية.. اعتقل أخي مرة أخرى.... قيل إن كل من شارك في الانتفاضة سيعدم. كانت أمي خائفة جدا.. ذهبوا جميعا ليكونوا مع أمي ..أتاني المخاض وأنا وحدي في البيت.. سمعت صرختها الأولى.. الثانية.. لم اسمع الثالثة ، كان الحبل السري قد التف حول عنقها واختنقت.

طحنا الحصار الاقتصادي، فضاق العراق بنا.. قررنا الرحيل. سلمنا كل أموالنا لصديقنا لتحولها إلى الدولار.. حتى اليوم لم نر تلك "الصديقة".

استأجرنا منزلا في بغداد وعشنا هناك..

بعد ثلاث سنوات، بدأت القوات الأمريكية حملتها" لتحرير العراق".

اطل علينا الصحاف وزير الإعلام حينها عبر التلفاز: "سنرد العلوج.. سننتصر على الأمريكان".. تمكن أولئك "العلوج" من احتلال بغداد في ثلاثة أسابيع......

تسعة وثلاثون صاروخا تهز سكون ليل بغداد، ساعة إعلان بوش الابن "تحريرنا"..

المرارة

All over our city people have painted religious slogans and pasted up posters of Imams to attract blessings and riches... sometimes because they are afraid of the religious parties controlling Basra

Um Mohammed, Souk Al Ashar, Basra

I walked into the market to buy a black abbaya and hijab...ever since I was a child, I've hated these things. These days I have to buy them for my daughter and persuade her to wear them! The religious militias will not leave her in peace if she walks in the street with her hair uncovered. Um Mohammed

يضع اهالي مدينتي على جدران بيوتهم ومحلاتهم شعارات دينية وملصقات للائمة ورجال الدين للتبرك وجلب الرزق احيانا .. وخوفا من الاحزاب الدينية المهيمنة أحيانا اخرى

ام محمد – سوق العشار – البصرة

ذهبت الى السوق لشراء عباءة سوداء .. لطالما كرهتها منذ كنت صغيرة . واليوم اشتريتها لابنتي . اقنعتها بارتدائها . اخبرتها ان لابد من ذلك؟ .. لابد من ذلك أقنعت ابنتي أن ترتديها ..أخبرتها أن لا بد من ذلك! المليشيات الدينية التي سلبت مدينتنا لن تتركها بسلام ان مشت في الشوارع بدونها . ام محمد

Khaled was twenty-three years old, he worked as a hairdresser in a salon opposite the Qouriya police station. A small truck stopped...the driver jumped out...got in another car and sped away. Khaled rushed out of the salon, shouting "car bomb, car bomb" to warn people in the square...then the place exploded. Nothing at all remained of Khaled except this picture, shown to me by his friend. Lu'lu'a, Kirkuk

خالد في الثالثة والعشرين، يعمل حلاقا في محل قبالة مركز شرطة قورية القريب. توقفت شاحنة صغيرة.. قفز سائقها.. صعد في سيارة أخرى وانطلقوا مسرعين. خرج خالد من محله صارخا: "مفخخة".. وانفجر المكان. لم يتبق من خالد سوى هذه الصورة يريني إياها صديقه. قبالة مركز شرطة قورية في مدينتي كركوك

Um Hussein lives in the bathroom of a secondary school. She's more than 70 years old and all her children have left her. Her only companions are her weak heart, her broken hip and her blindness. It is strange that she bears no anger towards either her children or her country. Noor, a secondary school in the Ashar area, Basra

The 'perseverance and courage' of Basra was used as propaganda by the former regime and now Basra's mourning of its children, killed and dumped in mass graves, is also being used as propaganda - this time to prove how fascist the former regime was. Either way, Iraqi people are erased from the picture and Basra's citizens are still grieving. Noor

تعيش أم حسين في حمامات مدرسة يزيد عمرها عن
السبعين عاما .. تخلى عنها أولادها يرافقها فقط قلبها
الضعيف..وركبها المكسور والعمى الذي تعانيه. الغريب
أن أم حسين ليست غاضبة على أولادها أو وطنها ..
نور - مدرسة ثانوية في حي العشار - البصرة

ومثلما كانت البصرة "الصامدة" جزءا من حملات النظام
السابق الدعائية، باتت البصرة الفجوعة بأولادها والمقابر
الجماعية مادة إعلامية تستغل لإثبات فاشية النظام
السابق.. في الحالتين غيّب العراقي ومازال الإنسان
البصري مقهورا .. نور

This is the Natural History Museum.
Our science teacher brought us
here on a school trip...the place
was full of stuffed animals and the
remains of ancient human beings...
after the occupation, everything was
destroyed...the building demolished...
Um Mohammed, Natural History
Museum Basra

The sound of bombs doesn't scare me as
much as their ugly words full of hatred.
They said "Death is closer to you than
your skin". That was the second death
threat I received. This time I got it in a
text message on my mobile. Noor and
I were taking pictures. I didn't tell her
about the message. I tried to hold myself
together and not collapse. Um Mohammed

هذا متحف التاريخ الطبيعي في البصرة.. أتذكر أن مدّرسة
العلوم اصطحبت صفنا لزيارة المكان كان ممتلئاً بالحيوانات
المحنطة وآثار الانسان القديم.. بعد الاحتلال حطم المكان
بأكمله. ام محمد – البصرة

لم تدخل أصوات المدافع ودوي القذائف والانفجارات الرعب
في صدري مثلما فعلت كلماتهم الممتلئة بالحقد والقبح..
أخبروني بقرب نهاية حياتي.. هذا هو التهديد الثاني الذي
أتلقاه، كان هذه المرة رسالة عبر الموبايل.. كنت ونور نصور
لم أخبرها بمضمون الرسالة.. أكملت عملي وأنا أطبق على
روحي كي لا أنهار .. ام محمد

Abu Zeinab is a very poor man...he carries his 10 year-old daughter, Zeinab, who has cancer...the illness granted us by the 'liberators' with their internationally prohibited weapons... Abu Zeinab took his daughter to Iran for treatment...he came back broken with pain...he didn't have $2550 – the price of Zeinab's treatment Um Mohammed, A Khaleej quarter in the Fao area, Basra

Bush (the father), called it 'Desert Storm' and Saddam Hussein, the 'Mother of All Battles', but we just called it 'Purgatory'. They filled my city with depleted uranium and now hundreds of our children suffer from the cancers that it causes. I wonder whether my daughter, my daughter's daughter or my daughter's daughter's daughter will suffer in the same way. I have a searing rage in my heart. Um Mohammed

أبو زينب رجل معدم.. يحمل ابنته المريضة ذات العشرة أعوام. زينب مصابة بالسرطان.. المرض الذي منحنا اياه "المحررون" بأسلحتهم المحرمة دوليا. اخذ طفلته الى ايران لعلاجها.. عاد يكسره الألم.. كان كل ما يحتاجه هو 2500 دولار فقط ثمن علاج زينب..
ام محمد - حي الخليج ، قضاء الفاو في مدينتي البصرة

بوش الأب سماها "عاصفة الصحراء".. سماها صدام حسين "أم المعارك".. ونحن سميناها أم المهالك. هذه الطفلة هي واحدة من مئات الأطفال الذين يعانون السرطان الذي تسببت به هذه الحرب. رؤيتها جعلتني أتساءل..هل ستعيش أبنتي.. أبنتها ..أو حفيدتهما نفس الألم. شعرت بغضب يتملكني .ام محمد

In my country we now prepare our graves, as we prepare a cradle to receive a new-born baby. Noor, the Hassan Al Basri Cemetery in Al Zubair, Basra

After the occupation, people started searching for their missing children. They looked in the security prisons, but didn't find anyone there. People said they could hear voices from cells underground. My father and brother went to see. They told us: "They were calling the missing people's names, beating on the ground – they put their ears to the concrete...they thought they heard knocking in response. They eventually managed to dig up the earth and break through. Of course, there was no one there". Noor

في بلدي نهيئ قبورنا كما نهيئ مهدا لاستقبال مولود جديد!!!. نور – مقبرة الحسن البصري – البصرة

بعد الاحتلال، بدأ الناس يبحثون عن أولادهم المفقودين بحثوا في سجون الأمن العام وعندما لم يجدوا أحدا ، قالوا انهم يسمعون أصوات تناديهم من أقبية تحت الأرض . ذهب أبي وأخي إلى هناك. اخبرونا بعدها " كانوا ينادون عليهم.. يطرقون الأرض.. يلصقون أذانهم عليها .. يصغون.. اعتقدوا أن أحدا ينادي عليهم بطرق مماثل..عندما تمكنوا في النهاية من ثقب الأرض . لم يجدوا أحدا بالطبع". نور

These boats provided a living for
5000 families...they used to fish
and sell their catch both inside and
outside Iraq. The port was flourishing,
economically vibrant. "Ever since the
beginning of the occupation, no one
in the Iraqi government has thought
to visit this area or to try to solve its
problems...to provide gas so the boats
can move...to clear the mud banks
from the water" said Abu Nour, head of
the port, with a despair and anger that
he couldn't hide. Um Mohammed,
the port of Fao, Basra

كانت هذه القوارب مصدر رزق خمسة آلاف عائلة،
تعيش من صيد السمك وبيعه داخل العراق وخارجه.
كان هذا المكان مزدهر اقتصاديا "منذ الاحتلال لم يفكر
أي من المسؤولين في الدولة العراقية بزيارة هذا المكان
وحل مشاكله.. توفير الوقود لتسيير السفن والقوارب..
كري المياه من ترسبات الطمي" اخبرني أبو نور، مدير
المرسى بأسى وغضب لم يستطع كبحه .. ام محمد - مينا.
الفاو – البصرة

When we were young the sky
Was clouded in winter
And the rain fell...
And every year, when the grass grows, we get hungry
Not a year has passed when Iraq has not been hungry
Noor, 'Song of the Rain', Badr Shaker Al Sayab (Iraqi poet)

Previous page
I went on a trip with friends...I was choked by the sight of
our palm trees...they'd been decapitated. The owner of the
boat told me that his father had died of grief over his palm
tree; he couldn't bear to see his life, the life of his father and
his grandfather torn up by the roots. In the war with Iran
in the 1980s, the palm trees were victims, in the 90s, during
sanctions, the poor of Basra sold their palm trees to the Gulf
States – cheaply. After the occupation, our palms are now
being burned – and I can't understand why. Noor, Basra

منذ أن كنا صغارا كانت السماء ،
تغيم في الشتاء
ويهطل المطر . .
وكل عام –حين يعشب الثرى– نجوع
ما مر عام والعراق ليس فيه جوع .
انشودة المطر – بدر شاكر السياب

الصفحة التالية
صدمني منظر نخيلنا مقطع الرؤوس. أخبرني صاحب القارب أن والده مات حزنا على
نخلاته، لم يحتمل رؤية حياته.. حياة آبائه وأجداده.. تجتث هكذا ببساطة. الثمانينات،
الحرب مع إيران، النخل كان ضحية. التسعينات، الحصار، باعه فقراء البصرة إلى الخليج
بأثمان بخسة. بعد الاحتلال، نخلنا اليوم يحرق ولا يمكنني أن أفهم لماذا!! نور – البصرة

Basra is a port sitting on a sea of oil...It was always fertile ground for agriculture. Despite all of this we live in extreme poverty. Everything is polluted – dirty quagmires of sewage and rain – The greater the destruction around us, the more we fear one another and the harsher the looks we give each other. Noor, Basra

البصرة ميناء يعوم على بحر من النفط... كانت دائما أرضا خصبة للزراعة. برغم كل هذا، نعيش في فقر مدقع.. كل شئ ملوث .. الشوارع المدمرة المهملة، طفح المجاري، والأمطار المتجمعة، أكوام القمامة. كلما ازداد الدمار من حولنا، ازددنا خوفا من بعضنا، وازدادت قسوة النظرات التي يرمق بها بعضنا بعضا. نور / البصرة

When the US army invaded, they closed off most of the major roads. The concrete barriers and barbed wire have become an essential part of the architecture of our Baghdad. Before the occupation, this was a huge, crowded bus station where everyday thousands of people travelled in and out of the city. Lujane, Al Alawi area, Baghdad

I went to see my friend at Mustansiriya University. I was horrified to see pieces of human flesh hanging in the palm trees. The day before, a man had blown himself up near a van taking female students to the college...as people rushed to help the wounded, a car bomb exploded killing rescue workers...and a few minutes later yet another car bomb went off, killing anyone who was still alive... Lujane

عندما دخل الأمريكان قطعوا معظم الشوارع الرئيسة وصارت الحواجز والأسلاك الشائكة جزءا من "معمار" بغدادنا .. قبل الاحتلال كان هذا المكان محطة كبيرة لمغادرة ووصول الاف الناس يوميا من بغداد واليها .

لجين- منطقة العلاوي – بغداد

ذهبت لزيارة صديقتي في الجامعة المستنصرية .. صدمتني رؤية بقايا اشلاء الضحايا على النخيل .في اليوم السابق فجر رجل نفسه جنب باص لنقل الطالبات . سارع الناس لانقاذ الجرحى فانفجرت سيارة اخرى قتلت المسعفين ايضا بعد دقائق قليلة انفجرت سيارة اخرى وحصدت من بقي حيا .. لجين

التسلسل الزمني

شكل من أشكال المقاومة

انا مخرجة افلام مقيمة في لندن،عراقية الاصل. حين اتصلت بي يوجيني لاول مرة صيف عام 2006 حول تصوير مشروع العدسات المفتوحة في العراق، كنت قد انجزت فيلمين وثائقيين آخرين عن العراق.

وصلت الى دمشق في شهر كانون الاول عام 2006 برفقتي كاميراتي وما من كادر عمل غيري. بدأت التصوير وسرعان ما ادركت أن تناول يوجيني للموضوع كان مختلفاً، فمنذ البدأ أكدت على اهمية الجانب الوجداني في الصورة. صحيح انك يجب ان تتعلم الاضاءة والتركيب ولكن بدون عواطف ومشاعر تصبح الصورة الفوتوغرافية مجرد لقطة. سعت يوجيني الى ان تجعل النساء يفكرن عبر مشاعرهن ليحددن ما تعبر عنه الصورة أو كيف جعلتهن تلك الصورة يشعرن وان يكتشفن غايتهن منتلك الصورة وما تعبر عنه.

كانت نقطة التحول هي خرائط الحياة. حين بدأت النسوة المسحورات بالاصغاء الى بعضهن،أخذت قصصهن وتجاربهن تقترب من السطح واخذن بأدراكها وإعادة تشكيلها . وبالنتيجة كانت كل واحدة منهن تمسك بخيط حياتها وسوية قمن بحياكة نسيج التجربة الجماعية للنساء العراقيات خلال العقود المنصرمة. كانت العملية ملئ بالنشاط والتغير ضمن اطار مشروع ابداعي حيث يتم انجاز شئ ما يمكن ايصاله للأخرين. أن العمل الذي انجزته المشاركات كان متميزاً لقوته ووضوحه الوجدانيين.

خلال فترة حرب الخليج عام 1991 وكحال الكثير من العراقيين في الخارج امضيت الليالي ليلة بعد ليلة امام شاشة التلفزيون اتابع "الالعاب النارية" وانفجارات سماء بغداد في العتمة والقنابل "الذكية" تصيب اهدافها كما لو كانت في احدى العاب الفيديو. ذعرت الى درجة فقدت فيها قدرتي على الكلام باللغة الانكليزية التي تكلمتها طيلة حياتي. فقدت الكلمات معانيها وصرت اعاني لأتذكر اسماء ابسط الاشياء، المنضدة، الملح، الشباك... من الممكن ان يكون ما فقدته هو قدرتي على الحديث عن الخسارة... والقدرة على النعي، في حقيقة الامر. بالتالي استعدت صوتي عن طريق اخراج فيلم عن العراق وبدأت ادرك آنذاك انك احياناً تحاول ان تصلح بعمل ابداعي ما هدم على ارض الواقع.

انا على يقين انه كان شكلاً من أشكال المقاومة فبالنسبة للنساء بالتقاطهن للصور وكتابة نصوصهن المرافقة وبالنسبة لي بأخراج الفيلم. كان تأكيداً للوجود بوجه كل الدمار الحاصل داخلنا وخارجنا.

ميسون الباچتچي
لندن 2010

وصلنا إلى البصرة وقبل سفرنا بثمانية عشر ساعة اتصلت هناء لتخبرني بأنها غير قادرة على السفر لان أخيها الذي يعيش في بغداد قد هجر من بيته فلم يجد من مكان سوى بيت أهله في البصرة ومن ثم فان انضمامها إلينا صار أمرا مستحيلا. وبينما كنت على وشك الاستسلام لفكرة سفرنا بدون مشاركة من البصرة سوى نور رشح لي الصديق موفق الرفاعي ساجدة أم محمد التي ما أن قابلتها حتى شعرت إنها هي من كنا نبحث عنها طوال الشهرين الماضيين .

نعم لم أكن أنا من وجدهن.. كُنَ هُنَ من وجدنني لتقول كل واحدة منهن قصتها وتمضي. تحفرها في كلمات وصور في أيامنا التي أمضيناها معا.. سروة وأم محمد توفين واختتمت قصصهن بينما ما تزال الأخريات يكتبن نصوصهن في بلد يندفع بقوة نحو الاندثار...

إرادة الجبوري
اسطنبول 2009

النحت بالصوروالكلمات

ابنتي تنام في فراشها وأنا اجلس إلى طاولة الكتابة في قلب مدينة ساحرة الجمال والهدوء، استنطق امرأة تدعى إرادة تعيش في بلد اسمه العراق 2006 و2007. تقول لي: لا أريد أن أضع الحياة في تابوت اللغة بالرغم من أني سعيت لكي نقول ما يجب أن نقوله في ذلك الزمان والمكان..

حسناً، أكان علينا الكلام في زمن لم يكن هناك من صوت غير صوت الرصاص وعصف السيارات المفخخة وهدير الطائرات المقاتلة و الساسة بمليشياتهم ووسائل الإعلام وهي تُصَيِّرنا أرقاما تمحى مع كل نشرة جديدة وأرقام جديدة؟ هل هي الشجاعة التي دفعتنا لأن نتكلم؟ لا ، لم تكن شجاعة.. كان الخوف هو من جمعنا سوية.. الخوف من أن تمضي اللحظة مثلما مضت غيرها خلال عقود من الزمن من دون أن نقول ما حدث والخوف من أن نكون ذوات تحكي عن ذاتها لا عن تجربتنا الجماعية للآخر، الآخر الممسك بسلطة الكلام في لحظة تاريخية ما. أمضيت شهوراً في البحث عن مشاركات. بعد أن قدم صديقي يحيى الكبيسي لأهالي مشاركتين من الفلوجة ضمانات حول شخصي كان على تقديم المشروع لهن ولأسرهن وشرحه وتقديم ضمانات لعدم ارتباط بأي جهة سياسية او تمويل مشبوه . تم كل هذا في أيام معدودة عبر خطوط هاتفية دائمة الانقطاع. دخول الفلوجة تلك الأيام محظور على غير أهلها. كدت افقد أعصابي وأنا اكتشف مصادفة إن صلاحية جواز سفر مريم تنتهي قبل سفرنا بأسبوعين . كان علينا تجديد جوازها وهذا يعني استخراج وثائق جديدة بعد أن احترقت وثائقها في معركة الفلوجة الأولى في نيسان 2004 – و بعد ذلك كان علينا ان نجد وسيلة لايصال الوثائق إلى بغداد.

انضمت نيران إلينا بعد أن رشحتها صديقة جارتي لمى التي تعيش في كركوك. تعرفت عليها وعلى أسرتها واستعدت للسفر معنا بعد موافقة عائلتها. لكن فقدان أختها ذات العشرين عاما وابن أختها البالغ من العمر خمس سنوات في حادث انفجار عبوة ناسفة في سوق شعبي قتل كل رغبة بالحياة لديها. فرشحت لي الصديقة نرمين المفتي لؤلؤة لتنضم الينا .

سافرت إلى الموصل وأنا احمل هوية مزيفة دعوت الله أن لا اضطر لاستعمالها . انخلع قلبي هلعا وأنا أرى بيت صديقتي الدكتورة بشرى البستاني بأبوابه ونوافذه المخلوعة من جراء عصف سيارة مفخخة انفجرت على مبعدة شارعين من بيتها في اليوم السابق لوصولي . كان من المتفق عليه أن تقدمني لمشاركة و أسرتها لكني شعرت بالحرج والفظاظة من وجودي في وقت عصيب. أبعدنا شظايا الزجاج عن زاوية في المطبخ وأمضينا الليلة نشرب الشاي متلفعات بالبطانيات ونحن نحتضن المدفأة النفطية ونستعيد رحلتنا المبتلة المتلئة مفارقات إلى بيروت عام 1992 متجنبات الحديث عن العنف الذي يجتاح العراق مثل بلدوزر فقد كابحه. عدت فجرا إلى بغداد من دون أن أقابل أسرة بتول .. كان ذهابي أليهم لا معنى له من دون من يقدمني إليهم ويطمئنهم حول شخصي خاصة وان أخبار الاتجار بالنساء، أصبحت حديث وسائل الإعلام.

هن من وجدنني ولست أنا من وجدهن لأني لا أملك تفسيرا آخر لترددي باختيار سروة. حاولت ايجاد نقطة تلتقي فيها توقعات كل واحدة منا عن المشروع. في ثالث مكالمة أخبرتني إنها لا تعرف التوقف عن الحلم وإنها لا تحلم من اجلها فقط بل من اجل أمها أيضا. اقنعتني كلماتها لأتمسك بها بقوة واطلب منها أن ترشح لي شريكة لها في العمل من الموصل فاختارت أنطوانيت التي سرعان ما حظت بقبول وارتياح .

تعرفت على لجين في خضم انغماسها بهجوم لفظي على رجل في جامعة بغداد لم يجد ما يقوله غير التزام الصمت، بعد أيام رايتها فقدتها إلى غرفتي بالكلية. عرضت عليها المشاركة فوافقت ورشحت لي سراب التي اتصلت بها من مكتبي وكانت حينها منشغلة بصبغ جدران بيت أخيها الذي تسكن فيه ..

ثلاث نساء من البصرة كانت لديهن الرغبة للمشاركة وتغيرن لأسباب شتى: في النهاية عثرت على نور عن طريق والد احدهن. نور بدورها عرفتني على هناء الحلاقة الشابة التي تعمل بصالونها برغم كآبة البصرة بميليشياتها. أخذتني هناء ، من صالونها بسيارتها الخاصة لمقابلة والدتها الأرملة. كانت أم هناء مترددة في الموافقة خوفا من ردود أفعال أعمام هناء وأخوالها الذين لن يوافقوا على سفرها بدون مرافقة شخص من الأسرة.فطرأت على ذهن هناء وأمها أن تخبرا الأسرة أن هناء ستسافر بمعية أسرة صديقة كان من المخطط فعلا أن تذهب إلى دمشق لزيارة السيدة زينب وكذلك لشراء جهاز تاتو والتدرب عليه لكي تستعمله في صالونها. وعدتها بان اساعدها واستعنت بريا لترتب أمر تعلم هناء التاتو في دمشق خلال ساعات الفراغ ...

شتاء 2006 كان الناس يغادرون بغداد بشكل لا سابق له وكانت حجوزات الطيران تحتاج إلى شهر سابق بالقليل. غادرت المشاركات من كركوك والموصل من مطار اربيل، وفضلت المشاركتان من الفلوجة السفر برا على القدوم لبغداد والسفر منها بينما لم يكن من حل أمامنا نحن مجموعة بغداد غير التوجه جنوبا إلى البصرة للسفر إلى دمشق من هناك .

الى أخريات بهذا المدى من التنوع الاجتماعي والديني والسياسي. كنت متوترة وخشيت ان تتحول الحوارات الى مجادلات مشحونة. إلا انه ورغم بعض لحظات التوتر حاول الجميع ابداء الاحترام للمقابل. راقبت وجوههن إذ يصغين الى الاخريات. وجوه يملأوها الصبر والتعاطف.

كنت قد عشت في الشرق الأوسط ولكن ما من شئ كان ليشفع لهذه القصص التي سمعت. كل ما كان في ذهني عن العراق اصبح في مهب الريح. لم يكن لدي ادنى فكرة عن مدى قسوة التجربة العراقية في العقود الثلاث الماضية. لم يسلم أحد من الخسائر الكبرى التي يصعب الحديث عنها والفواجع ولم يتح لأي كان الفرصة للتشافي والتقاط الانفاس بعدها.

كان عليهن ان يقمن بدراسة عوامل مختلفة للتصوير ويتجولن في أزقة المدينة العتيقة ليصورن ويراجعن لقطاتهن فيما بعد حين يعرضنها. كانت هنالك ضرورة ملحة لاتقان كافة تقنيات التصوير لغرض استخدامها للتعبير عما يرغبن بقوله.

وحين حان موعد العودة كانت كل واحدة منهن قد اختارت موضوعها الذي ستصوره. اختياراتهن جاءت صريحة وشخصية. على الصعيد اللوجستي، سألناهن كيف سيقمن بحماية انفسهن وتقليص المخاطر، فأجابت العديدات: سأترك ذلك لأرادة الله." فضجنا بالضحك حينها. لم يكن هذا ما توقعت سماعه. ولكن وجهة نظرهن كانت في غاية الوضوح. عندما ينهار العالم من حولنا، فرغم كل الاحتياطات والاستعدادات التي نعدها، إلا اننا في الاخير نكون بلا حول ولا قوة.

من بين العراقيل التي تم اجتيازها بشجاعة خلال الاسابيع الستة الاولى كانت التهديدات بالقتل (ليس بسبب المشروع) والخطف من قبل الميلشيات والتفجيرات وحظر التجول وغلق الحدود – ناهيك عن قطع الكهرباء وقطع الطرق وطوابير البنزين وانقطاع المياه وشبكات الهواتف التي كانت جزءاً من الحياة اليومية.

رغم كل ذلك فعندما حان الوقت لتحرير القصص عادت النساء الى دمشق في مجاميع صغيرة بمعيتهن اعداد هائلة من الصور التي قمن بتحريرها وكتابة قصصهن عبرها خلال ورشات عمل استمرت خمسة ايام.

قصصهن هي الشاهد الفريد من نوعه على الانسانية المخفية خلف تقارير الاخبار حيث البشر يتحولون الى اعداد. هذه القصص هي شهادة على شجاعة اولئك النسوة اللواتي مررن بما لا يخطر على البال من ذعر نتج عن اجتياح العراق.

اتوجه بالشكر لـ
Index on Censorship
لدعمهم الخالص وبرنامج التنمية التابع للامم المتحدة
UNDP
لتمويلهم للمشروع
Prince Claus Fund
وتلك المانحة السخية التي آثرت عدم ذكر اسمها لتمويلهم لتمويلهم طباعة هذا الكتاب.

وكذلك اتقدم بالشكر لمديرة المشروع في سوريا وهي في نفس الوقت المترجمة وصديقتي العزيزة نوارة محفوظ وليسون الباجقجي التي اخرجت فيلماً عن المشروع ولدعمها وصداقتها اللتين لا يقدران بثمن والتي غيرت طبيعة المشروع الى حد ما. وشكري كذلك لأرادة الجبوري التي بشجاعتها وقوتها الهمت الجميع.

ولا يفوتني ان اشكر كل من ساهم في انجاح المشروع والذين لا يسعني عدهم أو تسميتهم. إمتناني القلبي للنساء اللواتي جئن من العراق لرواية قصصهن. أكتب هذه السطور في ذكرى اثنين منهن: ساجدة ام محمد التي فقدناها بسبب تأثيرات اليورانيوم المنضب وكذلك بسبب المنظومة الصحية المنهارة في العراق. وفي ذكرى سروة التي قتلت على يد جماعة مسلحة تستهدف النساء الناشطات.

يوجيني دولبرگ
طهران
2010

مقدمة

في اعقاب 2003 اصبح العراق يفتقر الى حكومة فاعلة والى بنى تحتية مدنية. اضحى الناس اكثر عرضة للعنف العشوائي من قبل اولئك الذين استغلوا الفوضى شر استغلال. بحلول عام 2006 كان عدد كبير من الصحفيين اما قتل او استهدف او اختطف حتى كاد ان يستحيل العمل واقتصرت مصادر المعلومات من داخل العراق على العسكرية والحكومية. وغابت عن الاسماع قصة الناس العاديين.

آنذاك كنت اقطن سوريا المتاخمة للعراق. كنت قد عملت لسنوات عديدة قبل ذلك في انحاء مختلفة من العالم بصفة مصورة. استفزني تزايد الطبيعة التجارية للاعلام. كان المطلوب قصص لا تمت بصلة لدوافعي للعمل او حتى نوع التصوير الذي يجذبني. من جهة اخرى كنت أحس اني محظوظة لاتصالاتي اليومية مع العديد من الاشخاص الرائعين. وكلما مر الزمن وانا خارج اوربا والولايات المتحدة كلما ازددت ادراكاً لمدى التدخل، في شؤون البلدان الاخرى مما يفقد الناس احساسهم بعائدية تاريخهم اليهم وكذلك يفقدهم دورهم في تحديد مسار بلدانهم ومستقبلها. صرت على يقين بعطب وضيق الفكر الذي يحدد السياسة الخارجية والتنمية. فأن الانظمة التي على اساسها تجمع المعلومات ويتم تفسيرها كانت عقيمة حسب فهمي. فعلى اي اساس يكون التقييم الذي يضعه اجانب زائرون لاسابيع وجيزة افضل من الفهم الذي لدى الناس من ابناء البلد لمجتمعهم؟

في دمشق التقيت بالعديد من العراقيين الذين فروا من بلدهم. ولطالما اذهلني مدى العنف الذي تعرضوا له والطبيعة السريالية لذلك. والى اي مدى اضطر الناس للتحمل من أجل البقاء على قيد الحياة. شمر أحدهم عن اكمامه ليريني اسمه وعنوانه ورقم هاتفه موشمة قائلاً إن قتل وألقي بجسده في الطريق أو تعرض لانفجار او قطع رأسه سيتمكن من يجده من ارجاع جثمانه الى اهله. واضاف ان ما عمله ليس بالجديد وان العديدين فعلوا فعله.

وكذلك طرق اسماعي مراراً وتكراراً الحديث عن شجاعة وبسالة وجلادة النساء العراقيات ونشاطهن. ففي غضون 26 عاماً من الحروب المستمرة و 13 عاماً من ابشع العقوبات عبر التاريخ تمكنت النسوة في العراق من ادامة تماسك المجتمع فيما كان رجالهن في ساحات القتال. هن من كن يكسبن لقمة العيش وهن من حافظن على وحدة العائلة هذا كله تزامن مع الضغط النفسي للتعايش مع جيل من الرجال العراقيين الذين افنوا زهرة شبابهم في الحروب. فمنذ عام 2003 حاربت النسوة العراقيات للحفاظ على حقوقهن الدستورية التي لم يظفرن بها الا بعد جهد جهيد والتي حاولت الاحزاب الدينية المحافظة ان تبدلها. هي حقوق بديهية تخص الميراث والزواج والطلاق وحضانة الاطفال.

في لندن واسوة بالملايين تظاهرت ضد الحرب فبصفتي مواطنة بريطانية احسست بوطنة ما كانت حكومتي تفعله في العراق وكذلك احسست بواعز المسؤولية للمساعدة في تدوين ما كان يحدث. فقررت اقامة مشروع تدريبي للتصوير يحمل اسم عدسات مفتوحة في العراق مع مجموعة من النسوة العراقيات. لم يكن هدف المشروع التقاط صور جميلة وخلابة بل صور تعبر عن مشاعرهن وعن توصيل تجاربهن وليست فقط عن الاحداث الدائرة.

اتذكر اول مكالمة هاتفية لي مع ارادة الجبوري المديرة العراقية للمشروع من بغداد والتي اخذت اجازة من عملها لاجل ان تعمل على المشروع العدسات المفتوحة وكان عليها ان تتحمل اعباء ومخاطر السفر في ارجاء البلد مستعملة عدة هويات ومتنكرة احياناً للعثور على النساء اللاتي شاركن في المشروع قائلة: " هذا ليس بمشروع، انه حلم اريد ان اعيشه لاجل ابنتي لكي تحيا وتفهم ماهو دائر الان على حقيقته."

لم يُتح لنا ان نعقد المشروع في العراق الا ان سوريا كانت بديلاً موائماً. فهناك اتيح للنساء ان يتلقن فن التصوير ويشاطرن تجاربهن قبل ان يعدن الى العراق لالتقاط الصور لكتابة قصصهن المصورة.

سكنا وعملنا سوية في بيت دمشقي في المدينة العتيقة. جاءت النسوة من كل انحاء البلاد دون خبرة مسبقة في التصوير. أدركت انه بدأ وقبل الشروع بالقصص المصورة، إحتاجت النساء الى الحيز والثقة والوسائل الابداعية ليكون بمقدورهن تصوير حياتهن. فأخذت بسرد قصة حياتي لهن وتجربتي الفردية التي جعلتني ما انا عليه اليوم رغبة مني في ابث روح المساواة والثقة والانفتاح بينهن.

لن انسى ما حييت ذلك الصباح الذي فيه طلبت منهن ان يرسمن خطوط حياتهن وعيونهن مغمضة. عزفت انغام العود الرقيقة في ارجاء الغرفة. في ايديهن اقلام وعيونهن مغمضة. انشحنت الغرفة بالمشاعر اذ أخذن بأستذكار كل لحظة في حياتهن وكيف أثرت تلك اللحظة على مسار حياتهن. سرت حول الطاولات، أرقب وجوههن وأجسادهن اذ تتغير بتغير الخط الذي يرسمنه. أيديهن تتشنج وتتصلب مع هبوط الخط نحو الاسفل - إذن ثمة ذكرى مريرة - واكتافهن وجباههن تنفرج مع استذكار الاوقات البهيجة. كل واحدة منهن كانت معزولة في ظلمتها لا يقاطعها الا صوت خريشة القلم الماضي على الورق ليذكرها بوجود الاخريات حولها. ومن دون كلمات رأيتهن يتنقلن عبر الحروب والعقوبات والزواجات الفاشلة واللوعة والحب والسعادة واوقات المقاومة والانجازات والانتصارات الصغيرة. وبالتالي افضت هذه الخطوط الى خرائط حياة كاملة تزينها قصائد وملاحظات واقوال مأثورة وصور شخصية. طلبت من كل مشاركة ان تقدم خارطة حياتها للمشاركات الاخريات. ورغم ان معظم المشاركات قد عشن معظم الوقت في العراق، ألا انها كانت المرة الاولى التي يستمعن فيها

هذا الكتاب يضم مجموعة من الصورة الفردية وثماني مقالات مصورة لنساء من بغداد والبصرة والفلوجة وكركوك والموصل في عام 2006 و2007. هؤلاء النسوة لسن مصورات ولا كاتبات وإنما جمعتهن حاجتهن لتوثيق قصصهن.

Published in Great Britain in 2010 By Trolley Ltd
www.trolleybooks.com

Photographs and texts ©
Photographers / Open Shutters/ Index on Censorship, 2009

Introductory texts ©
Irada Al Jabbouri, Eugenie Dolberg, Maysoon Pachachi

Creative Direction: Eugenie Dolberg, Gigi Giannuzzi
Art Direction and Design: www.fruitmachinedesign.com
Text Editing: Eugenie Dolberg, Maysoon Pachachi, Hannah Watson
The right of Eugenie Dolberg to be identified as the author of this
work has been asserted by her in accordance with the copyright,
designs and patents act 1998.

A catalogue record for this book is available from the British Library.

ISBN 978-1-904563-99-0

Printed in Italy 2010 by Grafiche Antiga

This project was made possible by the dedicated support of Index on
Censorship and funded by the UNDP, Ministerio de Asuntos Exteriores
Y de Cooperacion and Agencia Española de Cooperacion Internacional.

This book received generous support from the Prince Claus Fund

For information about the exhibition, Open Shutters Iraq,
please contact eugeniedolberg@gmail.com

For information about a feature-length documentary film,
'Our Feelings Took the Pictures: Open Shutters Iraq'
by Maysoon Pachachi
please visit www.oxymoronfilms.com

OPEN SHUTTERS

عدسات مفتوحة

* * T R O L L E Y * *